JOURNEY
INTO
NOW

Other books by Leonard Jacobson

Words from Silence
Embracing the Present
Bridging Heaven & Earth

JOURNEY INTO NOW

Clear Guidance
on the Path
of Spiritual Awakening

LEONARD JACOBSON

CONSCIOUS LIVING
PUBLICATIONS

CONSCIOUS LIVING
P U B L I C A T I O N S
150 Camino Al Barranco
La Selva Beach, CA 95076

First printed in March 2007.

Printed in the United States of America.

10 9 8 7 6 5 4 3 2 1

Library of Congress Control Number: 2006909908

ISBN 978-1-890580-03-2

Library of Congress Cataloging-in-Publication Data

Jacobson, Leonard 1944–
Journey into Now: Clear Guidance on the Path of
Spiritual Awakening/Leonard Jacobson

For Mary,
whose love and devotion
inspires me every day.

And for

Rachmat,
Halimah,
Fran,
Stephen,
and
Claire,

whose loving support
has helped me share this teaching.

And for

the many students and seekers of truth
who have been willing
to reveal themselves fully.
It is your courage and honesty
that has allowed me to see deeply
into the human soul and
witness the magnificence within.

To each and every one of you,
I love you. And I thank you.

CONTENTS

Introduction

The fact that you are reading this book means that you are ready to be liberated from the limited world of the mind into the infinite and unlimited world of Now.

This book is a comprehensive guide to your awakening, and when you do awaken, you will discover a world more sacred and beautiful than anything you could have imagined.

In this book, I share with you how to still your mind in the simplest way, and how to become fully present and awake in the truth of life. I show you how to arise in mastery of the mind and ego, so that you can remain fundamentally present in your day-to-day living.

Presence enhances every aspect of your life, including your relationships. It is immensely worthwhile.

As an essential part of my guidance into the present moment, I speak of past lives and the soul's journey. I speak of God and the eternal dimension of life. I speak of the need for healing, forgiveness, and repentance. I speak about the right expression of emotions. I speak at length about the ego and how to free ourselves from its tyranny. I even speak about death.

But let me assure you that everything I speak of is directed towards only one end. How do we free ourselves from the past and awaken fully into the present moment? How do we awaken out of illusion into the truth of life? How can we be restored to Oneness and yet still live our lives effectively within the world of time?

I urge you to approach each page of this book in innocence. I have not written this book for your mind or ego. It is written for that dimension of you that is already awake, has always been awake, and will always be awake. I am addressing the dimension of you that is eternal.

Each page reveals a part of the mystery. It is like a road map home. I suggest that you read it carefully in its entirety and then, from time to time, randomly open it. You will find hidden keys to awakening on every page.

This book has the power to liberate the sleeping giant within. If you truly embrace what is written here, you will awaken.

Author's note

Some of the names mentioned in this book have been changed to protect the privacy of those involved.

*THE JOURNEY IS FROM
HERE TO HERE.
AND THE ONLY TIME
YOU CAN ARRIVE
IS NOW.*

*WE ARE ON A JOURNEY
OF BECOMING THAT WHICH
WE ALREADY ARE.
THAT IS THE IMPOSSIBLE
PARADOX OF OUR LIVES.*

Part 1

A CALL
TO
AWAKEN

The past is gone.
The future never arrives.
In truth, there is no life
outside of this moment!

I KNOW WHO YOU ARE!

I want to begin by saying that I know who you are. You are an eternal Being. You are love, acceptance, and compassion. You are strength, clarity, and truth. At the deepest level, you are pure consciousness, beyond form and content. You are powerful beyond imagining. You are an instrument of God's will upon the earth. You are a champion of God and your ultimate destiny is to awaken into Oneness. You are the champion of your own soul. It is through your awakening in this lifetime that your soul will be restored to its immortality. You are the redeemer of Oneness and the revealer of Heaven on Earth. You are Buddha, revealing the pure mind of God. You are Christ, revealing the pure heart of God. And you are Lao Tzu, revealing the way of God in the world. You are awakened man. You are awakened woman.

You are eternal but you are on a journey through time. Your journey has taken you from Oneness into duality. It has taken you into a world of illusion and separation. It has taken you from the present moment into the past and future. It has taken you from truth into a world of idea, concept, opinion, and belief.

The journey is purposeful but, for the most part, we have lost our way. We have forgotten who we are. We are now functioning as egos in our own private and separate worlds. We have strayed too far from the truth and we are following in the footsteps of the prodigal son.

Because of our technological advances, we have become too destructive to continue living unconsciously upon this earth.

It is time to awaken, but before we can awaken, we must recognize how and where we are lost.

THE DILEMMA OF HUMAN EXISTENCE

Most humans are living in a state of unconsciousness. Even though our eyes are open and we appear to be awake as we walk and talk and live our lives, in truth we are not awake.

We are lost in the mind, which is a world of the remembered past and the imagined future. It is a world of thought, memory, and imagination. It is a world of opinion, idea, concept, and belief. It gives us the sense of a life outside of the present moment. It gives us a sense of ourselves outside of the present moment. And that is the great illusion.

In truth, there is no life outside the present moment. In truth, you do not and cannot exist outside of the present moment. The world of the human thinking mind is an illusory world and yet almost everyone believes that it is real. It is as if we have fallen asleep and the life we are living is a kind of dream, from which we must awaken.

To awaken spiritually or to become enlightened is to awaken out of the past and future world of the mind into the truth and reality of the present moment.

It is not until you awaken and become fully present that you will realize that you have not been present. It is not until you awaken that you will realize that you have been asleep, dreaming that you are awake. To be enlightened is to awaken out of the dream. It is a profound and dramatic shift in consciousness.

Separation

The more we are caught in the mind with its endless chattering thought, the more we feel separate from the truth and reality of life revealed through the present moment.

At a subtle and unconscious level, we feel separate from the present moment and from each other. We feel separate from the true source of life and we feel separate from God. Almost all human endeavor is an attempt to deal with or escape from the feeling of separation which exists at the very foundation of our unconscious life.

Separate Worlds

When we are in the mind, we exist in separate worlds. There are as many separate worlds as there are unconscious people upon this planet. We get along with those whose separate worlds are somewhat similar to our own. We are at odds with everyone else.

But when we become present, we leave our separate worlds and come into the one world, experienced through the senses, in this moment of now.

There are no memories or imaginings to distort our reality. There are no concepts, ideas, opinions, or beliefs to distort our experience of what is here now. There are no philosophies or religions to separate us. Our minds are silent. I am silent. You are silent. How can the experience of silence differ for us? It cannot. In silence and Presence, we come together in Oneness.

THE EGO

When you are lost in the world of the mind, you are functioning as an ego and you are controlled by the ego.

Using a few simple words and phrases, let me sum up the basic attitude and position of the ego, as it functions within the world.

"Me! Me! Me!"
"Mine! Mine! Mine!"
"I'm right. I'm right. I'm right."
"How can I use this or make use of this?"
"What's in it for me?"

There are six billion egos living on this planet. Can you not see why the world is in such a sorry state? Can you not see why we are destroying Heaven on Earth for our own short-term gain? Can you not see why the tiger and the gorilla are facing extinction, along with countless other species? Can you not see why there is so much injustice, abuse, greed, cruelty, and inequality upon this planet?

We get along with those who share the same set of illusions. It is called *collusion*. They are our friends. We declare war on those who dare to believe in another set of illusions. They are our enemies. Religion, and particularly religious fundamental-ism, is the most obvious and dangerous example. Nationalism is another.

"Me! Me! Me!"
"Mine! Mine! Mine!"
"I'm right. I'm right. I'm right."
"How can I use this or make use of this?"
"What's in it for me?"

You can see that this basic attitude of the ego affects every aspect of our lives and relationships. It reveals so much about what is really driving our political and economic systems and our need for military might. Because we live unconsciously as egos upon this planet, there is every chance that we will render this beautiful earth uninhabitable for humans. It will not be the meek who will inherit the earth. It will be the ants and cockroaches.

It is time to awaken. We must awaken individually and then awakening will follow at the collective level. But we cannot awaken unless we face who we have become on this long journey through time and separation. We must own, acknowledge, and confess our egos if we are to be released from its dominance.

What is it like to be truly present?

To be present is to awaken into that dimension of yourself and life that transcends the thinking mind. You are silent and you are fully present with what is actually here now.

If you are fully present, there is no moment other than this moment. That is what it means to be awake in the truth of life.

At the very deepest level of awakened Presence, the past and future have disappeared and only this moment is available to you. You are awake in the eternal now. You cannot function within the world of time for the simple reason that there is no time. There is no sense of your self outside of this moment.

This does not mean that one who has awakened is always functioning at the deepest level of Presence. It is possible to function at a more superficial level of Presence so that the world of time becomes available. Even when you participate in the world of time, you are still deeply grounded in Presence and the present moment is always recognized as the truth of life.

If you are fundamentally awake in Presence, you live without judgment, fear, and desire. You live in a state of acceptance. You live as love in the world. The illusion of separation has dissolved. You live with a strong sense of the Oneness of all things, and a continuing awareness of the impersonal and eternal dimension of existence. You see others as equal and enlightened, even if they are unaware of it. This extends to animals and the world of nature. It is impossible for you to intentionally harm another. You are compassionate and you always act with integrity. You cannot be dishonest. There is something inside you which simply will not allow it.

When you are fundamentally awake in the truth of life, you are substantially free of ego motivations, desires, and reactions.

This is not to imply that one who is awake is somehow perfect. At times, you can react like anyone else, and experience fear and uncertainty, or feelings like hurt and anger. The difference is that now you know that you are caught temporarily in the illusion of separation. You do not believe in the story that is presenting itself to you. You know that the past is somehow projecting itself into the present. You do not identify with emotional reactions. And yet, you take full responsibility for whatever is arising. The experience is owned and accepted but not acted upon as if it is the truth.

Two possibilities

There are always two possibilities at any moment in your life. Either you are fully present or you are in the mind.

When you are fully present, you are in a state of consciousness called Presence. You are here now. You are experiencing the truth and reality of the present moment. The illusion of separation has dissolved and you are in a state of inner silence, relating moment to moment to that which is here now with you.

When you are in the mind, you have abandoned the truth and reality of the present moment for an illusory world. When you are in the mind, you are somewhere in the past or future. You are not here now. What you are experiencing is not real.

Using the power of thought, memory, and imagination, you have created a world of illusion and now you are condemned to live in it. Nearly all human suffering is attributable to this simple fact.

YOU ARE NOT HERE YET!

In working with many people over the years, one of the themes that I have consistently encountered is best expressed by the following exchange with one of my students. Diane, a woman in her mid-forties, had attended a number of my seminars and finally arranged to have a private session with me.

After sharing with me some of the difficulties she had been experiencing in her life, and after expressing some of the emotional pain she had been feeling, she finally got to the heart of the matter.

"I just don't want to be here," she protested strongly, in response to a question I had asked her.

I had heard this statement from many people over the past few years. It is a major obstacle to awakening, for awakening involves being fully here.

"Why don't you want to be here?"

Her reply was very clear.

"There is too much suffering here. It is too painful. It is too difficult."

Tears began to roll down her cheeks, as she opened up into all the painful feelings repressed within her. Her life had been a difficult one, filled with emotional suffering.

"I really don't want to be here," she sobbed.

"That is all very well," I replied. "But you are not here yet."

She looked puzzled.

"What do you mean? If I am not here, then where am I?"

"You were born, but before you could emerge fully into life, you left the world of here now and you entered the world of not here. You are not here yet and so how can you know whether or not you want to be here? I suggest that you reserve your decision until you are really here."

"I do not understand," she said. "If I am not here, then where am I?"

"At an early age, you entered the past and future world of the human thinking mind, and now you are lost there. The world of the mind contains within it all your past suffering. There is no suffering in this moment. You continue to suffer because you are caught in the memory of past suffering. You continue to suffer because you are lost in the mind. You are lost in the past."

Her tears had stopped. She was paying close attention to my words.

"You cannot know whether or not you want to be here until you are here," I told her. "When you do finally liberate your-self from the prison that is the world of the mind, and you are fully here in the truth of life, you will discover that this is Heaven on Earth. Your suffering will be over and then you will be so grateful to be here."

How do you enter the world of the mind?

You enter the world of the mind whenever you think. It does not matter whether it is a spiritual thought or an intelligent thought. Any thought will take you there.

I am not saying that thoughts should stop. I am not saying that thinking is bad. I am just saying that all thought takes you into the world of the mind.

You energize your thoughts through the power of belief. The more you energize your thoughts by believing in them, the more imprisoned you become within the world of the mind. The more you glorify your thoughts, the more you become lost in the mind.

In truth, there is no life outside of this moment. Sooner or later we will all have to surrender to that simple truth.

Leaving the present moment

We humans are in some difficulty because we don't know how to stop thinking. Isn't that true? How many people can stop thinking and just be here in silence and Presence? And if you cannot stop thinking, then you cannot be present, for all thinking takes you into the mind.

There is nothing wrong with thinking. There is nothing wrong with entering the world of the mind, as long as you know that you are entering a world of illusion, and you know that only the present moment is the truth of life. Then you can play in the world of time, with your thoughts, memories, and imaginings. Enjoy yourself, but be careful! It is easy to get lost there.

If you identify with any of it, or take any of it too seriously, you will separate yourself from the present moment and the truth of life. You will be abandoning God, love, truth, and the present moment for the illusory world of the mind, filled with distorted memories and false promises.

YOU CAN CHOOSE TO THINK

You can choose to think. You can remain present as you think. The fact that you are thinking is real. What you are thinking about is not. You would be quite amazed to know how little I think. I am not trying to stop thinking. I think when it is necessary to think, but beyond that I don't think.

UNINTENDED THINKING

If you are thinking, but you are not intending to think, then the mind is thinking by itself. The mind is thinking itself into existence and then you are caught in its world. You are a prisoner of your own mind and you cannot escape. There is a very effective prison warden. It is your own ego.

SILENCE

When you become fully present, thoughts stop and your mind is silent. You are not trying to stop the thoughts. It simply happens as you become present.

But there is an even deeper level of peace and silence waiting to emerge. As your mind becomes silent, an inner door is opened, allowing an infinite and eternal silence to emerge from the core of your Being.

This infinite and eternal silence is the very essence of your Being. It is your true nature. It is the essence of all existence. It is the eternal silent presence of pure consciousness. It is the *I AM* of you.

It is that dimension of you that exists in this moment and only this moment. It is that dimension of you that exists in Oneness. It is your Buddha nature. It is the Christ of you, which exists in Oneness with God.

IN THE SILENCE OF THE PRESENT MOMENT

In the silence of the present moment, there is no past or future. There are no thoughts, opinions, concepts, or beliefs. There is no judgment. There is no right or wrong. There is no good or bad. There is no condemnation and there is no salvation. There is no despair and there is no hope. There is no blame or guilt. There is no expectation or resentment. There is no fear or desire. There is no separation. There are no divisions or boundaries. There is only this moment of now.

In the silence of the present moment, there is no nationality. There are no religions. There are no beliefs, doctrines, or dogmas. There is no ownership, possession, or control. There is no success or failure. There is no outcome. There is only this moment of now.

A VAST BLUE SKY

When you are fully present and your mind is silent, you are in a state of pure consciousness. I would liken that to a vast and clear blue sky. Not one cloud in sight. When a thought arises, it is like a tiny cloud passing across a vast blue sky.

Do you think that tiny little cloud can obscure the sky? Of course not!

But if you get involved in that tiny cloud, by identifying with it, believing in it, or even trying to get rid of it, you will find yourself being absorbed into it. The vast blue sky will no longer be visible or available to you.

On the other hand, if you simply witness the thought as it arises, and you are neither for nor against the thought, then you will remain open to the vast blue sky.

If you continue thinking, so that suddenly there are thousands of tiny little clouds, then the vast blue sky will be obscured.

The sky does not disappear. It is always here, but your awareness of it has been obscured by constant thought. Now you are disconnected from it. Now you have separated yourself from your essential nature, which is pure consciousness, infinite, silent, and eternal, like a vast blue sky.

FROM THE GARAGE TO THE KITCHEN

In one of my teaching sessions, a man in his late sixties, who was quite intrigued by what I was sharing with the group, raised his hand to ask a question.

"How can I be present in my everyday life?" he asked. "How can I be present as I walk from the garage to the kitchen?"

He listened very carefully as I responded to his question.

"As you walk from the garage to the kitchen, be present and conscious in the movement of your body. Be present with what you see. Be present with what you hear.

By bringing yourself fully present in this way, you honor God and the truth of life, and so God and the truth of life will be revealed to you."

My words had taken him into a deep state of Presence. He was quite radiant as I continued.

"As you walk in Presence, you will feel peace and love and the deepest level of silence arising within you. There will be a feeling of reverence for everything that is in your moment-to-moment awareness. If you are fully present with everything that you en-counter, you will be an awakened Being on your walk from the garage to the kitchen. Your journey will be a sacred one."

THE DREAM

A woman was asleep and dreaming. In the dream, she was on a train and, whilst on the train, she lost her two suitcases. Her two suitcases were her only possessions and she was very upset that she had lost them.

She began going from carriage to carriage, searching for her suitcases. She looked everywhere. She asked everyone if they had seen her suitcases, but to no avail. No matter how hard she tried, she could not find them. She was becoming more and more anxious and more and more desperate. Her dream was turning into a nightmare!

Just then, a car drove past her house next to her bedroom where she was sleeping. The car sounded the horn and she began to awaken out of her dream. She was almost awake, when she remembered that she had not found her suitcases.

"I can't wake up yet," she thought to herself. "I haven't found my suitcases."

She was about to go back into the dream to continue her search, when it occurred to her that if she could only wake up, then she was not on a train and she had not lost her suitcases.

In that moment, she chose to awaken from her dream.
This parable reflects a fundamental truth about our own lives. As children, we came into a world where no one was truly present. We did not receive the unconditional love and acceptance we needed. We were not allowed to be ourselves or express ourselves fully, and some of us even suffered abuse at

the hands of those who were supposed to care for us.

Those unfulfilled needs and emotional wounds are our lost suitcases, and we will not awaken from the dream until we find them. We are still searching for love, acceptance, and approval. We are still searching for someone to be present with us. We are still trying to escape from the pain.

But we will never find what we are looking for within the dream. It is only when we awaken from the dream that we realize we are searching for something that was missing in the past. As long as the search continues, we are held in the very past that we are seeking to resolve. As long as the search continues, we will remain lost in the dream.

Lost in illusion

It is possible to spend a whole lifetime trying to solve problems, overcome limitations, or heal wounds that belong to the past and have nothing to do with the present moment. It would be much easier to awaken into the present moment, where those limitations and emotional wounds do not exist.

Projecting into the future

We remember a less than perfect past and project that imperfect past forward, hoping to create a better future. This perpetuates our imperfect past and locks us into a world of illusion.

BRING CONSCIOUSNESS TO THE DREAM

Some people want to awaken, but the dream will not allow it. If you are caught in the dream, share it. Expose it. Bring consciousness to the dream and it will begin to release you.

THE FIRST STAGE OF AWAKENING

The first stage in awakening is to acknowledge that you are not awake. The first stage in healing your pain is to acknowledge the pain. The first stage in liberating yourself from limiting beliefs is to acknowledge those limiting beliefs. The first stage in freeing yourself from anger is to acknowledge the anger. The first stage in freeing yourself from fear is to acknowledge the fear.

If you're not willing to acknowledge who you are right now, you will never be free.

And you have to acknowledge it all with love, acceptance, and compassion, and without any judgment.

THE IMPERSONAL, THE PERSONAL, AND THE TWO DIMENSIONS OF THE EGO

There are two dimensions of your essential self and there are two dimensions of the ego. I would like to clarify these distinctions before proceeding any further.

At the deepest level of your essential self, you exist as an eternal Being. At this level, you have transcended time and you have transcended all sense of yourself as a separate individual. You exist in Oneness with all that is. You are an infinite and eternal silent Presence of pure consciousness. It is the *I AM* of you. It is that dimension of you that exists in this moment and no other. There is no past or future. Your mind is silent. You are fully present with what is here.

It is the fully awakened state of consciousness. There is no expression. You are totally immersed in the moment of now. It is impersonal.

But then there is the personal dimension of you that derives from the impersonal and reflects your unique individuality. I could call it your personality, but in the purest sense.

The impersonal and eternal dimension of you is like the ocean. The personal dimension of you is like the wave. The wave is an expression of the ocean and each wave is uniquely individual.

At the personal level, you are still grounded in silence and Presence, but time is available to you. You can participate in the world of time, but you do not get lost there, nor do you become identified with experiences arising within the world of time.

Experiences come and go, but you remain fundamentally present, without fear, judgment, desire, or attachment.

You know that only this moment is the truth of life, and that each moment is continually renewing itself. Each moment is experienced fully and then released. Experiences do not accumulate and so the past does not accumulate within you, which leaves you available to the present moment.

You still have memories. You can still plan for the future, but you are not lost there. You remain fundamentally present, even as you play in the world of time.

At this personal level, you are expressing all the qualities of eternal Presence, including silence, peace, love, acceptance, compassion, clarity, and strength. You are uniquely individual and yet you are an expression of Oneness.

However, if you live with fear, judgment, desire, and attachment, the present moment is never experienced fully, nor is it released. This leads to the past accumulating within you, and as this occurs, you become absorbed into the world of the mind.

You become so involved in the past and the future, and so involved in your thoughts, that you disconnect from the present moment. You are defined by your past memories and future imaginings.

No longer the personal expressing the impersonal, you are functioning as an ego within a world of separation. You live in a remembered past with all its pain and limitations, and you project forward into an imagined future. You are no longer living in the truth of life.

You began as an eternal Presence of pure consciousness, beyond form and content. You entered into a complex maze of thought, memories, emotions, ideas, concepts, opinions, and beliefs and now you are lost there.

When you are lost in the world of the mind, you are functioning as an ego, in a personal sense.

But there is another dimension of the ego, which is transcendent of your individuality. It is that aspect of human consciousness which manages and controls your life within the world of time. It is the Custodian of the Separation. It is an entirely different dimension of the ego and it has no intention of releasing you from its world.

When you are functioning as an ego, you are controlled by the ego. You are subject to its authority and you live by its unspoken laws.

If you are to awaken, you will have to bring to consciousness all the ways that you are lost in the mind, functioning as an ego. You will have to bring to consciousness all the ways that the ego holds you captive in its world of separation.

FINDING YOUR WAY HOME

In the early stages of awakening, you will have blissful and profound experiences of the awakened state of Presence, but you will inevitably return to your mind. Your mind is the home in which you live. It is the home to which you have grown accustomed.

Occasionally, you will leave your home and visit the present moment but you will not be allowed to remain there. It is as if there is an imaginary elastic band attached to you that quickly snaps you out of the present moment and back into the past and future world of the mind.

However, as you deepen into Presence and become more grounded in the present moment, and as you bring more consciousness to the mind, a gradual shift begins to take place. The imaginary elastic band becomes stretched and loosened and you find yourself spending more of your time in the present moment. The ego will not be so insistent upon your immediate return.

This relaxation and surrender of the mind and ego continues, until one day, without warning or notice, your home has shifted from the world of the mind to the world of Presence. Now your home is in the present moment.

To be present is your natural state. You will still enter the mind to think, but when you have finished thinking, you will spontaneously return to the awakened state of Presence, which is your new home. The elastic band is now pulling you in the opposite direction. It is pulling you from mind to Presence.

When this shift occurs, you have passed through a major transformation in your life. You are now awake. You are in your true home, which is the world of now.

Part 2

A TWO-STEP DANCE OF AWAKENING

*Awakening is simple if you know the way.
The Way of Awakening I share has become
so refined over the years that it has been reduced
to two simple steps. I call it the two-step
dance of awakening.*

THE FIRST STEP ~ PRESENCE

The first step in this two-step dance of awakening is to choose the present moment as the truth of life. More and more each day you choose to be present, rather than absent. This means that you will have to choose to be present many times each day. The more often you are present, the more the dimension of Presence opens up within you.

The only reason you choose to be present is that you know that the present moment is the truth of life, and you are choosing to be in the truth of life, rather than lost in a world of illusion.

THE KEY TO BEING PRESENT

Being present is remarkably simple. There is a key that liberates you from the prison that is the world of the mind, and releases you fully into the present moment. It is a simple key that I have been sharing with my students for many years now.

Gently remember to bring yourself present with that which is already present. That is the simple key to liberation.

When you are in the world of the mind, you are somewhere in the past or future. The one place you are not is in the present moment. So all you have to do is bring yourself fully present with something that is actually here in the moment with you. You will then emerge from the past and future world of the mind and enter into the world of now.

If you can see it, hear it, feel it, taste it, touch it, or smell it, you can be present with it. It is of the present moment, and so it brings to you the opportunity to be present with it.

When you first wake up in the morning, spend a few minutes before getting out of bed just being present in your body as it breathes. When you are having a shower, be present with the warmth of the water and the fragrance of the soap. Be present as you eat your breakfast. Be present as you wash the dishes. Washing the dishes can be a sacred experience if you are present.

Look around the room that you are in. There is so much with which to be present. Be present with the sound in each moment. If you are moving, be present and conscious in the movement. Be present with whatever is here now.

There are many times each day that you can be present. When you notice that you have drifted off into the world of thought, memory, and imagination, bring yourself back to the present moment. As you choose the present moment, you will deepen into Presence and it will gradually reveal its hidden treasures. Eventually, you will be fully established in Presence, and God and Heaven on Earth will be revealed.

YOU CAN ONLY BE PRESENT WITH SOMETHING THAT IS ACTUALLY HERE NOW

You cannot be present in some abstract way. Presence is not about disappearing into nothingness. You can only be present with something that is actually here.

It does not matter whether it is a door handle, a chair, a tree, a flower, or a bird soaring through the sky. If it is here in the moment with you, it is extending to you the invitation to be present with it.

Responding to the invitation

How do we humans usually respond to the invitation into Presence? We ignore it! We are so imprisoned within the mind that we cannot remain present with what is here for more than a few seconds. We have very little interest in living in the truth of life. We are the dreamers, dreaming the dream.

What will it take to respond to the invitation and awaken out of the dream? There is so much here with which to be present. Every moment reveals abundance. Walk through the forest in Presence. Walk through the garden in Presence. Behold the vastness of the sky. Be present with the ocean. Be present as you wash the dishes or as you walk from the garage to the kitchen.

The truth is uncompromising

The truth is uncompromising. It does not accommodate your preferences. It does not adjust to your desires. Either you accept the moment exactly as it is, or you leave the moment in search of more. God has nothing to offer you other than this moment. The ego can tempt you with so much more.

A GENTLE REMEMBERING

I have said that the key to being present is to gently remember to bring yourself present with that which is already present. What do I mean by remember?

We assume that remembering is a function of the mind that takes us back to some event in our past. That is a misuse of the word. To understand what I really mean, you have to consider the word *dis-member*. To dismember is take something that is whole, cut it, and separate it into parts. To *re-member* is a reversal of that process. It is to bring the parts back into wholeness.

Anything that you can see, hear, feel, taste, touch, or smell in the present moment is one part. *You* are the other part. In your remembering to be present with that which is already present, the parts are brought together and wholeness is restored.

YOU CAN BE PRESENT WITH YOUR EYES CLOSED

You can close your eyes and be present with your body as it breathes. You can be present with the sound you hear, moment to moment. You can be present with the feeling of air upon your face or the chair against your back. You can be present with physical sensations within your body, like tingling or itching.

You can be present with feelings that arise, as long as you do not become involved with the story woven into the feelings. That would take you out of the moment.

You can be present with a thought arising as long as you do not get involved with the content of the thought. You can be present with a feeling of inner peace. You can be present with a feeling of expansion.

It does not matter what you are present with, as long as you are present with something that is actually of the moment.

A HUMBLE DOOR HANDLE

A humble door handle has more power to bring you present than all the spiritual books in the world, simply because you can be present with it. It does not take you into the world of the mind, filling you with spiritual concepts and practices. Its invitation into the present moment is immediate, and the only time you can respond is now.

BENEATH THE BODHI TREE

A man sat beneath a beautiful Bodhi tree and spent many months reading great spiritual works.

One day, the tree spoke to him.

"Why do you read books about Jesus and Buddha and Krishna?" asked the tree. "I hold the key to your liberation! Those books will inform you but they will not awaken you."

The man was quite startled.

"I do not understand," he said with a mixture of fear and excitement.

"The words in those books will take you into your mind," explained the tree. "They will energize your thinking process and then you will move further away from the present moment and the truth of life. You will take yourself further into separation."

"Please continue!" said the man, looking a little puzzled.

"If you will but choose to be fully present with me," said the tree, "then thoughts will stop and the past and future will disappear. You will awaken into Oneness and the truth of life. You will see that I am God in the form of a tree. Everything you are seeking in those books will be revealed to you, simply by you becoming fully present with me."

The man smiled.

"That is exactly what is written in these books," he said. "Obviously I am on the right track."

And he continued reading.

A WALK IN THE GARDEN

Go outside and begin to walk slowly around the garden. Be present with a flower and then a tree and then another flower. Be present with one thing at a time and yet have the sense of the whole garden being present with you.

The important thing is that you are authentic and sincere. You are sharing the gift of presence with the trees and the flowers and they are sharing the gift of presence with you. It is a sacred experience.

You can tell the trees or the flowers how beautiful they are if you want to. You can say how much you love and appreciate them. Or you can remain silent. Be very focused as you walk around the garden. See everything in perfect detail but without any thought.

If you are truly present during your time in the garden, you will begin to encounter the living presence of God in every flower and every tree.

Eating a meal

Close your eyes and become aware of your body as it breathes. Hear the sounds and smell the food. When you feel present, open your eyes and see the plates, the glasses, the cutlery, and anything else on the table in front of you. If you are sharing a meal with others, pass the food and water to each other very slowly and very lovingly.

Let there be a sense of timelessness, a sense of mystery.

With a deep sense of gratitude, begin to take the first mouthful. Move your fork very slowly to the plate and then very slowly to your mouth. Taste the food as if you have never tasted anything before. Let it be the first mouthful of food in your life. Savor each delicious taste. Chew slowly and consciously. Be fully present in your chewing. Be fully present in your sense of taste and your sense of smell.

You will be amazed by the sacredness of such a simple experience as eating a meal.

Conscious movement

If you are truly present, there is consciousness in your hearing, there is consciousness in your seeing, and there is also consciousness in the subtle movement of your body. Most people are simply not that present or conscious.

The true purpose of Tai Chi is to help you bring consciousness to your body and its movement. But you don't have to practice Tai Chi for ten years to accomplish this.

The next time you scratch your head or cross your legs, just be fully present in the movement. It sometimes helps to slow down. As you bring full consciousness and Presence into your body and its movement, you will begin to feel like a Buddha.

I am reminded of an ancient teaching story.

Buddha was sitting with his disciples, and there was a fly buzzing around his head. With a graceful movement of his arm, the fly was sent on its way. About five seconds later, Buddha repeated the gesture even more gracefully, but there was no fly present.

One of the disciples noticed.

"Excuse me, Master," he said. "The first time you gestured with your arm there was a fly there, but the second time you gestured, there wasn't. Please explain!"

Buddha was silent for a moment and then replied.

"I noticed that I wasn't fully Present and conscious in the first movement. I just wanted to correct it."

If you were as diligent and committed to being present and conscious as Buddha demonstrates in this story, you would awaken very quickly to your Buddha nature.

Most of us, however, are simply too lazy or distracted, and being present and conscious is just not that much of a priority for us. And so we do not awaken.

The choice

Each moment you have a choice. Will you be in the present moment in the truth of life or will you be in the illusory world of your thinking mind? With gentle remembering, you can choose to be present.

You are not trying to stop thinking. You are not trying to escape from the mind. You are not trying to become enlightened. You are making a choice to be present, simply because the present moment is the truth of life and you are free to make that choice.

As you choose the present moment, your mind will become silent. Relax into the silence. Deepen into Presence. Enjoy all that God has to offer you in this moment. Enjoy the fullness and abundance of this moment.

IF THOUGHTS INTRUDE

If thoughts intrude, simply acknowledge the fact that thoughts are arising. Allow the thoughts to be there, but do not get involved in them. If you bring consciousness to the thoughts, they will stop. Thoughts thrive in an unconscious environment. They dissolve into nothingness in a conscious environment.

The last thing you want to do is to try to stop the thoughts. It is thought trying to stop thought. It is just a trick of the ego to keep you out of Presence.

When thoughts arise, just witness how your mind is active, and then gently come back to something that is in the moment with you. If after a few moments or minutes, thoughts intrude again, repeat the process. Acknowledge the thought, gently disengage from it, and return to Presence.

As you deepen into Presence, it becomes easier to witness thoughts as they arise. If there is no judgment or energy of opposition, your ego will eventually relax and stop thinking.

Is thinking necessary?

If you add up the time that it's actually necessary and appropriate to think each day, you would probably find that it doesn't total more than twenty minutes. Sometimes, it will be more than that if you're busy at work, or you have a lot of things you must do that require mental activity. But if you pay close attention, you will see that most of your thinking is unnecessary. All it does is create anxiety, or keep you in some past memory or future imagining.

There are so many opportunities during the day to be present, without any need for thought.

Why do you need to be thinking when you're washing the dishes? Why do you need to be thinking when you're having a shower? Why do you need to be thinking when you're walking from the garage to the kitchen? You know how to walk from the garage to the kitchen. You don't need to think about that!

Talking to yourself

Whenever you think, you are really having a conversation with yourself. But who is speaking? Who is listening? What is the point of this conversation?

It is actually a form of madness, but because everyone is lost in thought, it seems normal.

If you saw someone walking down the street speaking out loud, you would declare them insane. When you walk down the street thinking, the only difference between you and that insane man is that you have learned to talk to yourself silently, and you call it thinking.

The next time you notice that you are thinking, and you did not consciously intend to think, try speaking the words out loud. Externalize the whole conversation. Don't judge it. Don't condemn it, and don't try to stop it. Just pay attention. It's highly amusing. You will never need to listen to the radio again. You have your very own talk show inside your head.

WITNESSING THOUGHTS

When you are sufficiently grounded in Presence, you can witness thoughts as they arise. You are not trying to stop the thoughts. You know that any attempt to stop thoughts reinforces the thinking process and takes you further into the mind. Neither for the thoughts, nor against the thoughts, you just see them for what they are.

THE THINKING MEDITATION

If thoughts persist, and you find it difficult to be present, do not struggle against that. Do not fight the thoughts. Just relax and go with the thoughts. Be in a relationship of co-operation with them. Sit down and do the thinking meditation.

For fifteen minutes, think consciously. Be present with each thought. Speak the thoughts aloud. Complete each thought.

Most likely, the thoughts will not persist beyond thirty seconds, but if they do, then just relax and enjoy the meditation.

You will be amazed by where the thoughts take you. You will be amazed at just how far they take you out of the present moment. You will be amazed by how irrelevant most of your thoughts are. You will be amazed by the random nature of your thoughts.

The key to stopping thoughts is a complete absence of conflict with your thoughts. Then it is very easy to return to Presence.

HONOR THE MOMENT

It does not matter how often you are present. Five minutes a day in pure Presence will transform your life. What matters is whether or not you honor the present moment as the truth of life. It is very intimate. You will have to find your own creative way of demonstrating to the present moment that you honor it as the truth of life.

It is like a love affair. The more you demonstrate your love and appreciation for the present moment and everything in it, the more it will open to you.

THE PRESENT MOMENT IS NOT AN ILLUSION

There are many spiritual traditions that maintain that the physical world we live in is an illusion. This is very unhelpful! The only way to be liberated from the mind is to be present with something that is here in the moment with you. If all of that is an illusion, then with what will you be present?

The confusion arises because, at the deepest level of Presence, form can appear to dissolve into light or pure energy. When this occurs, you are penetrating into the very essence of all existence. You are encountering that which transcends form. You are encountering pure consciousness, which is the source from which everything arises. This does not mean that form is illusion. It just means that form is the doorway through to this deeper level. That which is in form and that which transcends form are one and the same.

Another way of saying this is that God is both Creator and Creation. Bring yourself present with the Creation and you will know the Creator.

THE BODY OF GOD

Everything in physical form is the body of God. Bring yourself present with the body of God and you will begin to experience the living Presence of God in all things present.

To be present is simple

To be present and fully awake is simple. It is immediate. It requires no practice. It is a gentle remembering. But to remain present in your day-to-day life and in your relationships is not so simple. Most people can only remain present for short periods of time. It is not long before they are unwillingly pulled out of Presence, back into the world of the mind.

That is why the second step of this two-step dance of awakening is necessary. I refer to the second step as "doing the work."

Part 3

THE
SECOND
STEP

To be present is not enough.
You must also arise in mastery.

THE SECOND STEP ~ MASTERY

The first step leads to Presence. The second step leads to mastery.

If you are constantly and involuntarily pulled back into the mind's world of the past or future, then you are not free. You are not awake. In order to awaken fully, you will have to arise in mastery. You will have to become a master of your own mind and ego.

The second step involves bringing consciousness to all the ways that you are pulled out of Presence.

What are the hooks that pull you back into the world of the mind? What is preventing you from becoming permanently and fundamentally established in Presence? Until these questions are answered, how can you awaken other than for a few short moments every now and then?

For the sake of clarity, the second step is divided into four sections, for there are four significant reasons why you are constantly pulled out of Presence, back into the world of the mind. The first is the resistance of the ego. The second is denial of who you have become. The third is the repression of emotions from the past. The fourth is entanglement in others.

RESISTANCE OF THE EGO ~ THE FIRST OBSTACLE TO FULL AWAKENING

The first reason that it is difficult to remain fundamentally present in your day-to-day living and in your relationships has to do with the ego itself.

As I have mentioned earlier, there are two dimensions of the ego. When you are lost in the mind, disconnected from the present moment, you are functioning as an ego in the world.

But there is also that other dimension of the ego, whose role is to manage and control your life within the world of time. It is the Custodian of the Separation.

If you are to awaken, you will have to bring to consciousness all the ways that you are lost in the mind, functioning as an ego, and you will have to bring to consciousness all the ways that the ego holds you captive in its world of separation.

The ego is dominant in human life and its resistance to Presence is the primary reason that humanity is lost in a dangerous world of illusion. If you happen to discover the true way of awakening, which is through the doorway of the present moment, the ego will vigorously resist. It is afraid of what it does not know and it can never know the present moment. The ego can never be present. It does not want to be abandoned into eternal darkness, as you become present and awaken into the truth of life.

The ego is extremely skilled at seducing and deceiving you. It has a bag of tricks, which it constantly uses to tempt you out of Presence into the world of the mind.

THE FORMATION OF THE EGO

When you were born into the physical world you were fully present, even though you were only a tiny baby. However, you came into a world where most people, including your parents, lived and functioned within the limited world of the mind. To a large extent they were unconscious. They were not fully present.

As a result, you were hurt over and over again. Your needs were not met in a way that would have helped you to relax and feel safe. You got angry in an attempt to get what you wanted, but that too was not allowed.

It was all too much for you to bear, and so the ego came into existence to protect you from all these difficult feelings. Essentially, the ego is your protector. It is the overseer of your internal experience and it also is in charge of how you relate to the outside world.

Its first role in your life was to repress all the painful, unpleasant, and unsafe feelings, like need, hurt, and anger. Its intention was to minimize your experience of rejection, unworthiness, and isolation. It then developed strategies for coping in an unconscious world, where no one was truly present.

As this process continued, the past accumulated within you and you were slowly absorbed into the world of the mind, just as your parents were many years before you.

The ego began in your life as your protector, but in order to succeed, it had to be in control of every aspect of your life. The ego can only be in control of what it knows, and everything it knows is based on past remembering or future imagining. The one thing the ego did not know then, and does not know now, is the present moment. And so it resists any movement into Presence.

In order to carry out its role as your protector, it has to keep you in its world of separation. If you do become present, it will not allow you to remain there.

As you mature, the ego becomes stronger and more sophisticated and the distinction between the truth of who you really are and the ego becomes more and more blurred. After a while the ego thinks it is you, and so the game shifts from protecting you to protecting itself and its role in your life. It becomes addicted to power and control and it becomes very unwilling to surrender that control.

The ego has become so dominant in human life that it is now the main obstacle to human awakening.

A bag of tricks

The ego is extremely skilled at imprisoning you in the past and future world of the mind. It has a bag of tricks to tempt you, deceive you, or seduce you into its world of separation.

It keeps you in the past with the energy of blame, resentment, guilt, regret, and remorse. If you identify with any of these energies, or if you believe in their story, you will find yourself locked into a painful past. This is what the ego wants, so that it can sustain its control in your life.

But the ego's world is also the imagined future and it has a very simple but clever trick that has successfully enslaved almost every human in a future that never arrives. Can you guess what it is? It is the promise of future fulfillment! It creates within us desire and hope, which keeps us focused in the future and out of the present moment.

We are all like children who fall for this deception, and until we see through this simple trick and realize that only the present moment can fulfill us, we will never awaken.

Enlightenment in the future

The ego can also seduce us with the promise of enlightenment in the future. If you follow certain spiritual practices, meditate, read spiritual books, or visit spiritual masters, you will eventually awaken. This is a false promise. The only time you can awaken is now. And the good news is that the present moment continually re-presents itself to you. It never gives up on you. It is always bringing to you the opportunity to be present.

WATCHING THE EGO

If you want to escape the tyranny and bondage of the mind, then you will have to become very watchful of what your ego is doing. Don't be against the ego in any way. Just see it for what it is creating. You cannot stop it. All you can do is watch it and somehow see through it. This is what the ego wants. It will keep testing you until you arise in mastery and it can no longer deceive you or fool you. It is very subtle. It needs to know that you see through it.

It is impossible to be watchful of the ego unless you are sufficiently grounded in Presence. Otherwise, it is the ego watching itself. It is like a dog chasing its own tail. You will not awaken.

THE DISTINCTION BETWEEN AWAKENED PRESENCE AND THE EGO

It is essential to know the distinction between awakened Presence and the ego. There is a simple test of Presence. If you are truly present, your mind is silent. There are no thoughts. That is the test and it is not negotiable. Everything else is the ego.

If any thought is arising, that is a clue that the ego is involved. If you are observing yourself, that is the ego observing. If you are commenting on your spiritual progress, that is the ego commenting. It is still duality, which involves the observer and the observed.

In Presence, you are in Oneness. You have transcended duality. You are in silence. It is only from silent Presence that you can witness the ego. It is only from silent Presence that you can relate to your ego with love, acceptance, and compassion. It is only in silent Presence that you are utterly without judgment. If the ego detects any hint of a judgment, it will not release you.

THE EGO WILL NOT RELEASE YOU EASILY

The ego exists within a framework of thought. Its existence and functioning is based in the past. The pain and all the unfulfilled needs from your past justify the ego's role as protector and controller in your life.

If you become present, the past disappears and with it, the pain and the unfulfilled needs. Then, what is the ego's role in your life? If you awaken, the past that justifies the ego's existence is no longer here. Its position of authority is threatened and so it will resist Presence. It will not allow itself to be rendered purposeless.

There is another reason why the ego is afraid of the present moment.

As you become more fully present, you become more embodied and you begin to encounter all those repressed emotions from your past, which are stored within the body.

But this negates everything that the ego has worked so hard, for so many years, to accomplish. Its role, since early childhood, has been to repress all the painful feelings and run its strategies of survival until the moment of your death.

It will not surrender its role easily.

What is even more frightening to the ego is that, if you are fully present, thoughts stop. The ego exists within a framework of thought. Its world is the past and future world of the thinking mind. If thoughts stop, the ego feels like it is disappearing.

From your perspective, entering the present moment is like entering life. From the ego's perspective, it feels like death. It feels like it is going out of existence. And it is true, at least for those moments, minutes, hours, or days that you are fully present.

And so the ego will resist your movement into Presence. It will not allow itself to be taken out of existence. It will not allow itself to die.

YOU CANNOT DEFEAT THE EGO

As long as the ego believes that it will die when you awaken, it will not release you. As long as you judge the ego in any way or try to eliminate it from your life, it will resist Presence.

In many spiritual teachings, there is an implication that, with awakening or enlightenment, the ego is somehow annihilated. There is an implication that enlightenment leads to the death of the ego. This is most unhelpful. It is impossible to defeat the ego. No one in human history has ever defeated the ego. Not Buddha! Not Jesus! Not anyone.

RIGHT RELATIONSHIP WITH THE EGO

The ego thrives on resistance and judgment. It thrives on rejection and opposition. The only thing that will bring the ego to a place of relaxation and surrender is the energy of love and acceptance. All you can do is unconditionally love and accept the ego, with all of its little games, manipulations, and strategies of seduction and distraction.

You must bring to consciousness all the ways that the ego resists Presence and tries to seduce you into the world of the mind, and you must do so with love, acceptance, and compassion.

This is only possible when you are present.

When you are functioning as an ego lost in the world of the mind, you are seeking love and acceptance, but you are seeking it outside yourself. You are seeking it from others. You are looking in the wrong direction. You will not find what you are seeking from others.

The only way to receive unconditional love and acceptance is to turn within. The only relationship that will be truly fulfilling and healing for you is the inner relationship between the ego, which lives within time, and the Awakened Presence that emerges when you are fully present. In this inner relationship, there is a complete absence of judgment simply because, in the awakened state of Presence, there is no judgment.

As an awakening human Being, it is up to you to bring the energy of love, acceptance, and compassion to your own ego. As the ego surrenders its resistance, you will find it easier to remain present. There will come a transformational point in your life where thoughts stop completely and your mind is silent for extended periods of time.

THE EGO CANNOT AWAKEN

The more your ego tries to become enlightened, the more you will suffer, because the ego is attempting to achieve something that is impossible for it to achieve.

This is a very common mistake for almost everyone on the spiritual path. The ego is trying so hard to awaken. It is meditating daily, engaging in all sorts of spiritual practices, performing rituals, lighting candles, going to retreats, reading books, being with different teachers. The ego is trying so hard to become enlightened and it simply can't happen.

The ego can never be present. It can never be awake in the truth of life. The ego's world is the world of the mind. It is based in the past and projects into the future. Its very existence depends on thought. The ego's efforts to awaken simply take you further into the future and further away from the present moment.

But if your ego can see through its own dilemma and relax, it will release you out of the mind into Presence. The ego must stop trying to become enlightened. All effort must cease. All trying must cease. Then there is just a gentle relaxation into the present moment. Now you are here! You are awake, at least for those moments that you are fully present. That's how simple it is.

DENIAL OF WHO YOU HAVE BECOME ~ THE SECOND OBSTACLE TO FULL AWAKENING

Denying who you have become on this long journey through time and separation is the second reason that it is difficult to remain present in your day-to-day life, and in your relationships.

To the extent that you deny who you have become, you will be denied the truth of who you really are. To the extent that you deny who you have become, you cannot be established in Presence.

As an awakened Presence living upon this earth, you are silent, present, loving, accepting, and allowing. You are compassionate. You are utterly without fear or judgment. You are free of all the traumas and limitations of the past and you are free of all anxiety about the future. You are peaceful, still, and calm. You are clear and strong. You are empowered from within. You are responsive and spontaneous. You are grateful and generous, and you live in constant awareness of the extraordinary abundance of this world. You exist in Oneness and you feel the living Presence of God in all things present.

You walk lightly upon the earth and your life is a demonstration of integrity and grace.

When you are caught in the world of the mind, and you are functioning as an ego upon this earth, you have become something less than the awakened Presence I have just described.

Who have you become? Who have we all become?

We are needy, greedy, fearful, controlling, manipulative, jealous, resentful, angry, and blaming. We are filled with expectations, and we feel resentful when those expectations are not met. We are filled with judgment of ourselves and others. We are entangled in a remembered past and lost in an imagined future. We crave success and fear failure. We are hopelessly lost in each other. We are deeply involved in abandonment of responsibility, manifesting as blame and guilt. We are desperately out of balance in a world of duality. We fear death. We fear loss. We fear the unknown. We are attached to everyone and everything. We are even attached to our suffering. We feel unloved. We feel unaccepted. We refuse to feel our pain and so we inflict that pain on others as a way of avoiding feeling the pain ourselves. We are lost in a world of illusion, insisting that it is the truth. We use. We misuse. We abuse.

Who you have become is the doorway to who you really are! One of the most important keys to awakening is to own, acknowledge, and confess who you have become at the level of mind and ego. You cannot sidestep it. You cannot hide it. You cannot go around it. You cannot fix it. You cannot change it.

All you can do is look into the mirror. Life is a mirror which constantly reflects to you who you have become. Your relationships constantly reflect to you who you have become.

But you have to be willing to look. If you really look into the mirror, what will you see?

Are you a victim? Are you a blamer? Are you angry? Are you guilty? Are you full of fear?

Have you spent so much of your life pleasing others that you have forgotten who you are and what you want? Are you carrying around unhealed emotional wounds from your past, which you project onto the present moment?

What are the limiting beliefs you have about yourself, others, and life? These limiting beliefs determine to a large degree who you have become.

What are you like in relationship? Are you controlling? Are you manipulative? Are you honest? Are you caring and supportive? Do you know how to express love? Do you use others? Do you abuse others? Are you full of judgment? Are you full of expectation and resentment? Are you really a child dressed as an adult? Are you projecting your relationship with your mother or father onto your wife or husband? What are you like when you don't get your own way?

Do you allow yourself to feel your feelings? Do you express feelings responsibly? How do you avoid your feelings? Do you take responsibility for the feelings that arise within you, or do you blame others and hold them responsible?

You must own, acknowledge, and confess every aspect of who you have become, if you are to be liberated from the world of the mind. And you must do so without any judgment.

It is not difficult. Just be vulnerable. Be honest and authentic. If greed is arising, identify it. Own it. Confess it. Confess it to someone who will not judge you, and if you cannot find someone who will not judge you, then confess it to God, who exists at the very heart of silence within you.

"God, I just noticed the energy of greed arising within me. Wow! I really am greedy! I confess it before you, God. I do not judge it or reject it. I am simply acknowledging it. But now I am choosing to disengage from the energy of greed and come back to Presence. I will not allow the energy of greed to lead me further into darkness and separation. I am more awake now, God. I am much more present and so, from the perspective of Presence, I can easily see who I have become at the level of mind and ego."

It is the same with any aspect of who you have become. Notice when you are judging yourself or others. Notice the many ways that you control yourself and others. Notice how you need to be right. Notice how you have become a victim.

Whatever it is, own it, express it, confess it, and then disengage from it and return to Presence.

Who you have become is not the truth of who you are. And yet, you cannot awaken into the truth of who you are, unless you are willing to own, accept, express, and confess who you have become.

It is an interesting and challenging doorway that you must pass through if you are to become established in Presence.

REPRESSED EMOTIONS ~ THE THIRD OBSTACLE TO FULL AWAKENING

To the extent that you have emotions repressed within you from the past, you cannot be fundamentally present.

The repressed feelings are constantly being triggered, and when they are triggered, you are pulled out of the present moment into that past experience, which you then project onto the present moment. You are no longer in the truth of life. You have regressed but you are not consciously aware of it.

Even when the emotions are not triggered, they still filter through, distorting your experience of life.

The process of repressing feelings began in early childhood. As a child, you needed your parents to be very present with you, but that need was not met. In a very subtle way, you felt isolated and separate. You needed your parents to be unconditionally loving and accepting and, for the most part, that need was not met.

Because your needs were not met, you felt hurt over and over again. And in response to feeling hurt, you became angry. You soon discovered that these feelings of need, hurt, and anger were either too much to bear or were simply not allowed, and so, with the ego's assistance, you began the process of repressing these feelings within you.

They gradually accumulated into reservoirs of repressed feelings held within the body.

Reservoirs of repressed emotion

There are reservoirs of repressed emotions stored within you. There is a reservoir of loneliness and isolation. There is a reservoir of unfilled need. There is a reservoir of hurt, sadness, and pain. There is a reservoir of repressed anger.

These feelings tend to leak through into your day-to-day living. They distort your sense of self and they adversely affect your relationship with others. Sometimes they are dramatically triggered. The dam bursts and you are flooded with feelings that have absolutely nothing to do with the present moment. Some people are constantly flooded with past emotions and their lives are full of unnecessary suffering.

If you are feeling lonely, it is a signal that it is time for some companionship. That is all it means. It does not mean that you have to find someone and get married. As a responsive and awakened adult Being, you would simply call a friend and meet for lunch. It is just a tiny feeling of loneliness, which invites an appropriate adult response.

But if that tiny feeling of loneliness triggers a release from the reservoir of loneliness and isolation dammed within you, you are suddenly overwhelmed with childhood feelings. Instead of calling a friend, you withdraw. You are convinced, at an unconscious level, that you are unloved and unwanted. You feel like a failure. You feel ashamed and you hide out, hoping that no one will see you like this.

It is the same with feelings of hurt and anger. The feeling of hurt is an indication that you are not getting what you want or you are getting what you don't want. Anger indicates the same thing. You are meant to respond to these feelings by calmly and lovingly asking for what you want or stating clearly what you don't want.

But if these feelings are flooded with hurt or anger from the past, you can no longer respond appropriately. No longer an adult who is present, empowered, and responsive, you are a hurt child reacting as you did in childhood, either by withdrawing and sulking, or by becoming very angry and full of blame and resentment.

You will have to empty these reservoirs of repressed emotions so that you can deepen into Presence and remain fundamentally present in your day-to-day living and relationships.

EMPTYING THE RESERVOIRS

If you are to awaken and become permanently established in Presence, you will have to reverse the process of repression. You will have to allow all the emotions repressed within you into conscious and responsible expression.

It is not difficult and it should not take very long, once you learn the art of being fully present and once you come into right relationship with your feelings.

For the next few days, before you get out of bed in the morning and before you go to sleep at night, say the following prayer:

"Beloved God, all I ask is to deepen into Presence, love, truth, and Oneness. If there are any emotions repressed within me that act as an obstacle to my deepening into Presence, love, truth, and Oneness, please orchestrate my life in a way that will trigger these emotions, so that they will surface into conscious and responsible expression, for healing, completion, and release."

When emotions arise, it is important that you do not try to get rid of these feelings. You are simply inviting them to arise and express authentically.

The feelings will surface with a story from the past. Allow the story to emerge, but do not believe in it.

It is as though you are playing two parts.

On the one hand, you are needy, sad, hurt, angry, or blaming and you express it fully and authentically. On the other hand, you are fully present as the feelings arise. You are witnessing the whole event as it emerges from within you, and you know that it has nothing to do with the present moment. You know that it is simply the past emerging for completion. If anything, you are mildly amused by the whole experience.

This is not therapy. You are not trying to fix anything or get rid of anything. You are simply correcting that earlier decision you made as a child to repress difficult feelings. You are restoring to the feelings their right to exist and express.

But as an awakening Being, you will do so responsibly. Anger expressed responsibly leads to laughter. If sadness arises, then cry. It will soon pass and be replaced by joy.

FEELINGS THAT ARISE IN THE MOMENT ARE YOUR FRIENDS

It should take about three months, and certainly not more than twelve months, to empty out those reservoirs of repressed emotions completely. Then you will be able to enter into an entirely new relationship with feelings that arise in the moment, and have nothing to do with the past.

Feelings that arise in the moment are your friends. They are messengers. They tell you how to respond appropriately to whatever is occurring in the moment.

If you are feeling hungry, eat! If you are feeling thirsty, drink! If you are feeling lonely, call a friend! If you are out with friends and you feel overwhelmed, leave. Get some space! There is nothing complicated about it. Your feelings are clues and signals about how to respond, moment to moment.

So respond, rather than react. It is very simple, as long as there are no repressed emotions flooding in from the past to distort your experience of the present moment.

ENTANGLEMENT IN OTHERS ~ THE FOURTH OBSTACLE TO FULL AWAKENING

To be awakened means that I am freed from my past and future and released into the present moment. It also means that I am freed from entanglement in others and released back to myself. How can I know who I am if I am entangled in you? How can you know who you are if you are entangled in me? We must free ourselves from our entanglement in each other if we are to awaken.

What do I mean by entanglement in others?

If I want you to love me or accept me, I am entangled in you. If I want you to approve of me or agree with me, I am entangled in you. If I am trying to please you to gain your acceptance, I am entangled in you. If I fear your judgment or disapproval, I am entangled in you. If I am afraid of being rejected by you, I am entangled in you. If I manipulate or control you, I am entangled in you. If I assume responsibility for you, I am entangled in you. If I judge you, blame you, or resent you, I am entangled in you.

The truth is we are all hopelessly entangled in each other. We are all hopelessly lost in each other.

GIVING AWAY YOUR POWER

If someone likes you, approves of you, or accepts you, you feel good. You feel uplifted. You feel worthy. But if they do not like you, approve of you, or accept you, you collapse. You feel unworthy. In this way you have given away all your power. You have become hopelessly entangled in others.

RELEASING YOURSELF FROM ENTANGLEMENT IN OTHERS

To free yourself from entanglement, you will have to bring to consciousness all the ways that you lose yourself in others.

Each time you notice that you are seeking love, acceptance, or approval from another, you will have to own, acknowledge, and confess that you are giving away your power. If you are trying to please another to gain acceptance, own, acknowledge, and confess it without judgment.

Anger expressed playfully and responsibly can be a liberating force in reclaiming your power.

ANGELA AND THE PLEASING OF MEN

One Thursday evening in Marin, I had just finished speaking about awakening and the need to be true to yourself, when I noticed someone weeping. It was an attractive woman in her early forties, named Angela.

"Just let it come up," I said. "That's fine. Just let it come up."

Through her tears, she looked up at me.

"What are the tears about?" I asked her.

"My father," she replied.

"What about your father?"

"I spent years trying to please him. He was so cruel."

"Were your efforts successful? Did you finish up pleasing him?"

"No!" she replied, with some measure of despair.

Her issue was immediately clear. She had learned to give away her power and her sense of self by trying to please her father and gain his acceptance and approval. It is one of the main ways that we lose ourselves and become disempowered. It develops into a pattern of entanglement, which can be very difficult to dissolve.

"If your father were here, what would you like to say to him, after so many years of trying to please him, without success?" I asked her.

"I have tried to please you, but I can't do it. I can't do it."

She was pleading and her voice was that of a victim.

"That is not what you would say if you want to liberate yourself," I told her.

"I tried! I tried really hard!" she said in an attempt to find the right words.

Once again her tone was pleading and helpless.

"That's not it!" I said, rather directly.

It began to dawn on her that she had been this way with all the men in her life.

"I was married for twenty years and it was impossible to please my husband, no matter how hard I tried. And my most recent relationship has ended. He just suddenly left."

"Did you try to please him?" I asked.

"Yes," she answered through her tears.

Her crying turned to sobbing. She was feeling the deep pain of not feeling loved by the men in her life, no matter how hard she tried to please them and win their approval.

I persisted with my questions.

"What do you say to a man, after spending so many years trying to please him, and you still can't win his approval? What do you say to him?"

"I love you but it won't work! It won't work," she said sobbing.

"No! That's not it," I replied dryly, showing as little compassion as possible.

"I tried so hard."

"No, that's not it."

I looked out at the audience.

"I wonder if it's worth sitting here for a couple of hours until she gets it," I said to them playfully.

Everyone laughed, including Angela. When the laughter settled, she tried once again, this time without any prompting from me. She was determined to get it.

"I can't please you," she said with some determination.

"Nope, that's not it."

She tried again to find words that might empower her.

"I don't know how to please you," she offered tentatively.

A deep sigh arose from within the audience. They were dying to interject with their suggestions.

"That is not it!" I said. "I will give you two more minutes to get to it and then we are going to finish. If you don't get it,

I will most likely send you off for twenty-five years looking for the answer. And you will be in one relationship after another, trying to please your man, but never succeeding."

"No. I've got to get it!" she protested.

"I'll ask you the question once more. What do you say to someone who you cannot please, no matter how hard you try? What do you say if you want to empower yourself?"

"You're impossible to please?" she said, looking at me in the vain hope that that might be an appropriate response.

The room erupted into laughter.

"No!" I said firmly.

She tried again.

"I can't please you. I don't know how to please you. I'm not going to please you."

"Pathetic!"

She was at a complete loss. She obviously did not have a clue. I looked out at the people in the audience.

"Okay, shall I give her a clue?" I asked them.

The response was a resounding "YES!" I looked back at Angela.

"Okay. I'm going to give you a clue."

She was looking at me with eager anticipation for a clue that might free her from this dysfunctional pattern from her childhood, which she had projected into all her relationships with men. I paused for a moment for dramatic effect and then I gave her the clue.

"Two words!" I said.

Her eyes lit up. At last she knew what to say.

"Fuuuuuck yooooou!" she said.

She said those two simple words of liberation with such power and force that, had they been in the room, her father, her ex-husband, and her most recent boyfriend would have been knocked down like three pins in a bowling alley.

"There you go!" I said, congratulating her.

She received a standing ovation and the applause was almost drowned out by the laughter. She looked deeply relieved.

"Some final guidance before you go back to your seat," I told her. "You gave your power away by seeking the approval of others. You have to reclaim your power. You have to reclaim yourself.

Anger will liberate you. These two words will liberate you. God gave us these two words so that we could express our anger authentically. Otherwise the anger will build up and turn inwards, further disempowering you.

You will have to learn the art of expressing anger playfully and responsibly. So practice saying these two words silently to every man you see, even as you walk along the street, or when you are in the supermarket! It doesn't matter whether you know them or not. Just keep on cursing until you are done. Okay?"

Once again the room erupted in laughter and applause.

RECLAIMING YOUR POWER

To free yourself from others, you will have to embrace the following statement:

"I am here for me, not you!"

At first, it might seem selfish but it is a necessary step in your process of liberation. You must reclaim your power and your right to exist independently of the judgments, opinions, needs, and expectations of others.

If you embrace the above statement fully and joyfully, it will lead you to a deeper truth. The statement, "I am here for me, not you," will lead you to the statement, "I am simply here."

That is the true liberation.

THE PRICE OF FREEDOM IS TO ALLOW FREEDOM

If I want to free myself from entanglement in you, I must allow you complete freedom. This means that you are free to agree with me or disagree with me. You are free to like me or dislike me. You are free to love me or hate me. You are free to accept me or reject me.

You are who you are and you are free to relate to me in any way you like. In fact, if you love me or hate me, that is a statement about you, not me.

If you judge me, I allow you that freedom. It is really none of my business. The energy of judgment is arising within you. You are the one who has to live with it. If you judge, it means that you still feel judged. If anything, I would feel compassion for you, for you are still caught in the energy of judgment.

If I want to be free, I must not violate you with my expectations, fears, or desires. I must not control or manipulate you in any way. I must not judge you.

To further disentangle myself, I must bring to consciousness how I assume responsibility for you, or expect you to assume responsibility for me. So many of us are lost in abandonment of responsibility. As I own, acknowledge, and confess all these dysfunctional patterns that entangle me in others, they will gradually dissolve.

The outcome will be freedom. No longer entangled in each other, we can enter into the deepest levels of love and communion. The irony is that we must separate from each other in order to realize Oneness.

THE WAY OF AWAKENING REVIEWED

To awaken, you will have to choose to be present many times each day. You will have to honor the present moment as the truth of life. You will have to know that everything outside of this moment is an illusion, created through the power of thought, memory, and imagination.

You can play in the world of illusion, but be careful not to get lost there.

When you are fully present, you are an awakened Being, at least for those moments that you are present. To be present is instantaneous and immediate. Just be present with what is here. There is no practice. There is no process. Either you are present in this moment, or you are not.

But to become fundamentally established in Presence, in your day-to-day life and in your relationships, you will have to go through a process.

If you are to be forever free from imprisonment within the world of the mind, and free from the bondage and tyranny of the ego, you must arise in mastery. This means that you will have to bring consciousness to the many ways that you are pulled out of Presence.

Bring conscious awareness to every subtle movement of the ego. Identify every strategy created by the ego to confuse you, seduce you, trick you, and hold you captive within the world of the mind.

Bring conscious awareness to every aspect of who you have become on this long journey through time and separation, and do so with love, acceptance, and compassion.

Release emotions that are repressed within you, by allowing them into conscious and responsible expression. Free yourself from entanglement in others. Transcend judgment of yourself and others.

There isn't anything that can be left in the darkness of your unconscious mind. You will have to turn over every stone in your quest for awakening. That is what true awakening is! You are fully present in the moment of now, and you are a master of your own mind and ego.

Part 4

THE
NATURE
OF
THE MIND

Riding on the wings of thought,
you enter the world of time.
Riding on the wings of thought,
you enter the world of the mind.

THE MIND

The mind is a state of consciousness. It is a kind of cyber space into which you enter whenever you think. It is a world of illusion. It is a world of separation. When you are in the mind, you are somewhere in the past or somewhere in the future. The one place you are not is here now.

A REMEMBERED PAST

The mind, by its very nature, is of the past. It is made up of the sum total of your past experiences, together with all your concepts, ideas, opinions, beliefs, attitudes, and judgments.

The mind and ego can only know things from the past, which it accesses through memory. It then projects that past onto the present moment. This distorts the reality of the present moment and renders it impossible for you to experience the truth of life.

To function at the level of mind creates a certain feeling of comfort and security. It gives you a sense of who you are, and it gives you a sense of what your life is all about. But it reduces everything to that which is already known, and it deadens you to life.

When you are experiencing life at the level of mind, in a very subtle way, you are saying to whatever is present:

"I already know you. I have already experienced you. I already have my opinions, judgments, and beliefs about you. And so I do not have to be present with you. I do not have to know you in this moment because I already know you from the past." There is no innocence in that. There is no presence in that. There is no life in that.

Not only does your mind contain all your memories of this lifetime, but it contains significant memories from all your previous lifetimes. It also contains the collective memory of everyone who has ever lived before you. The mind is an awesome instrument. Enter into it at your own risk. It is very easy to get lost there.

AN IMAGINED FUTURE

When you are in the mind, you are not only in the past. You are also in the future, but it is an imagined future.

At a subtle and often unconscious level, you remember the pain and limitations of the past and all the emotional traumas and unmet needs. Using the power of imagination, you try to create a better future. But the future you imagine is not the true future. It is the past projected forward. You then lock yourself into the very past that you are trying to escape.

As you dream and desire your way into the future, you might even create some good feelings, because your imagining carries with it the promise of hope. But it is a false promise. It never delivers. The future in which you believe never arrives. It will never fulfill you. Only the present moment can fulfill you.

By projecting into the future, you leave the present moment and imprison yourself in the world of the mind.

THE CREATION OF ILLUSION

When you are in the mind and the world of thought, then you are the creator, but what are you creating? You are creating your own world of illusion. You are creating a world of memory, idea, concept, opinion, and belief. You believe that the world of the mind is real and then you are condemned to live in it.

All over the world, people are creating individual worlds of illusion. You get along with those whose illusory beliefs match your own. These people are your friends. There is little reason for conflict. But when your world of illusion does not quite match your neighbor's, then you are entering into hostile territory.

When you believe in your illusions as truth, then you would be willing to impose your illusory beliefs onto others. You would even be willing to wage war against those whose illusions do not match your own. You can justify all manner of crimes in the name of your illusions.

SHARED ILLUSION

All the major religions are examples of shared illusion. Some are more lost in illusion than others. There is a simple test. Which of the religions has most tried to convert others to their view? The greater the attempt at conversion, the greater is the distance from truth. It is a simple formula. It is not too difficult to arrive at conclusions. All you have to do is look through the history books. For those with ears to hear, let them hear.

THE MIND IS LIKE A COMPUTER

The mind is like a computer and, like a computer, it can only function according to its programming. It would be wise to identify how your mind is programmed and how those programs affect your life.

The programming of your mind commences in the womb and continues throughout your childhood. It begins with a feeling, which leads to an impression, which leads to a thought form, which leads to a belief. These beliefs form the basic programming of your mind.

UNCONSCIOUS BELIEFS

The beliefs that form in early childhood are about yourself, about others, and about life.

Suppose, for example, that when you were an infant or a young child, your mother and father were very busy and were not as available to you as you needed them to be. Perhaps they had two or three other children to attend to or they were too occupied with work, and so they were not really present with you.

As a result, you experienced feelings of abandonment and isolation, which gradually led to the formation of the belief that
you are not wanted, or that you are not loved, or that you are
fundamentally alone in your life.

If you believe that you are unlovable, you will attract into your
life those who are incapable of loving. And even those who
happen along who are very loving will suddenly find themselves being unloving towards you. The outer world has to
adapt to your inner world.

If you have a belief that the people who love you will leave
you, then sure enough, it will happen over and over again.
This belief often forms in childhood when parents separate or
when a parent suddenly dies.

These beliefs then influence every stage of your development
and continue into adulthood, affecting every aspect of your
life and relationships.

If your mother or your father was emotionally or physically
abusive, it will lead to an unconscious belief that others are
abusive and that life is not safe. Amazingly, you will attract
into your life those who will abuse you.

Your mind seeks to be validated in this way.

"See," it will say to itself, "I knew I was a victim. I was right
all along."

You had better become aware of your unconscious beliefs.
They are creating your experience of life. And as long as these

beliefs remain unconscious, there is no way to be released from them.

Here is a list of some of the more common beliefs about yourself, others, and life, which may have been programmed into your mind in early childhood and which might still be unconsciously determining your experience of life.

Which ones belong to you?

I'm not wanted. I'm not loved. I'm not lovable. I'm not accepted. I'm not good enough. I can't do it. I'm all alone. I'm separate. I'm abandoned. I can't depend on others. I have to do it on my own. It's not safe to trust. I have to be in control. It's not safe to relax. Nobody understands me. Nobody listens to me. I don't count. I can't express myself. It's not safe to speak out. I can't say no. I can't ask for what I want. I can't have what I want. I'm a nuisance. There must be something wrong with me. I can't cope. I'm not safe. Life isn't safe. It's my fault, I'm to blame. It's their fault, they're to blame. I'm stuck. I'm trapped. I don't want to be here. It's not safe to leave. I don't belong. I don't fit in. It's not safe to show my feelings. I have to hide my feelings. I have to be good. I have to do the right thing. I have to be nice. I must not upset others. I have to hide who I really am. I'm not worthy. I can't trust my own judgment. I can't trust my feelings. I have to be brave. I have to be strong.

Can you reflect upon how these limiting beliefs might have affected you in the past and might still be affecting you?

THE MIND AND REGRESSION

When you are in the mind, you are somewhere in the past. Generally, you are not too far into the past and so you can function reasonably well.

But this is not always the case. Sometimes you experience periods of stress, worry, and anxiety. Sometimes you feel upset, hurt, or angry. Sometimes you feel rejected or judged. Sometimes you feel needy or afraid.

What is happening in each of these situations is that you have regressed to a past experience, probably from your early childhood, and you are projecting that past experience onto the present moment.

If you could simply see that you have regressed to a past experience, then there would be no problem. You would know that what you are experiencing has no foundation in reality.

In a very real sense you are dreaming, and the moment you realize that you are dreaming, you can wake up out of the dream. Once you identify the nature of the dream, it is easy to awaken.

THE EVOLUTION OF FEAR

In primitive times, fear was a primal feeling that arose within us whenever our physical survival was threatened. It was supposed to move us to fight or flight in order to survive.

If you encountered a saber tooth tiger, you would hardly sit around and think about it. The feeling of fear would move you immediately to fight or flight. As a primitive man or woman, your survival depended upon your response to the feeling of fear.

Fear has played a large part in the survival of the species. And fear still has a role to play in our current lives, if our physical survival is threatened. If someone attacks you with a knife, fear is meant to provoke a response of fight or flight.

But as we became more sophisticated, and moved more and more into the mind and its world of thought and emotion, fear entered inappropriately into that arena.

The fight or flight response was activated whenever we felt emotionally threatened. If someone criticized, judged, or rejected us, we perceived that as a threat to our survival and entered into a fight or flight response. This fight or flight response gradually develops into a pattern of behavior or a way of being in the world.

Those who, in childhood, were inclined towards flight as a subtle response to emotional pain, tend to become withdrawn and isolated in their adult lives. Life can be very difficult for them. They are over-sensitive and often feel like victims. They are afraid of anything that might lead to the feeling of being judged or rejected, because unconsciously those feelings are experienced as a threat to their survival. They are lost in seeking acceptance and approval.

Those who, in childhood, were inclined towards fight as a response to emotional pain, tend to become aggressive, competitive, controlling, and sometimes violent or abusive.

These patterns distort our experience of life and affect our relationships. It is important to bring them to consciousness. The truth is that emotional pain is never a threat to your survival. If someone criticizes, judges, or rejects you, it really has nothing to do with you. It is a statement about them, not you.

A BIRD'S EYE VIEW OF THE MIND

Awakening into the present moment gives you a perspective that was not available to you before. It gives you a bird's eye view of yourself. It enables you to become watchful of yourself at the level of mind and ego.

Until you awaken to a higher level of consciousness, there is no way to be watchful. Until you awaken, all self-knowledge is the ego trying to understand itself. There is no perspective that transcends the ego. It will not lead to liberation.

How THE PAST INTRUDES INTO THE PRESENT

Recently, I had a private session with a woman in her early forties. She shared with me that she was experiencing a lot of fear and anxiety in her life and that she would often cry for no apparent reason. She was desperate to find a man, and yet she had no interest in the men who were interested in her. In fact, she reported to me that she was mostly attracted to men who were unavailable.

After speaking with her for about fifteen minutes and hearing some of the details of her childhood relationship with her parents, the central core of her problem was clear.

As a young child, she did not get the love and attention that she so desperately needed. She felt very lonely, and she did everything she could to attract her parents' love and attention, but to no avail. After a period of time, she became convinced that she was unlovable, that there was no one here for her, and that she was all alone.

She has spent her whole life trying to avoid these painful feelings of isolation and abandonment, and she has spent her whole life trying to find someone who will be here for her.

However, there are two problems built into this scenario, from which there is no escape.

The first problem is that no matter how much she tries to avoid the emotional pain buried within her, it is impossible to do so. The fear and the pain and the feeling of loneliness, although repressed, are very close to the surface and constantly filter through, affecting her sense of herself and her experience of life.

The second problem is that no matter how much she tries to get someone to be here for her, it does not work, because her childhood reality is that she is all alone.

We live our lives according to our unconscious beliefs. Our whole ego structure is built upon those beliefs. The ego quite literally will not accommodate a life that does not match those unconscious beliefs. That is why she is only interested in men who are unavailable. It matches her childhood belief that there is no one here for her.

"There is no way out for you," I told her. "There is no solution. The pain and the fear and the loneliness will never go away and you will always be alone."

My intention was to bring the repressed emotions to the surface. The only way to release ourselves from a painful past is to feel all the feelings that are repressed within us.

She began to cry uncontrollably.

"Just feel the feelings," I said. "Allow them up from the deepest level. Be here with your feelings, without trying to escape."

Her crying deepened. She began to wail like a baby.

"I am so afraid," she said as she wailed.

I allowed her some time to experience the feelings fully. After a few minutes, I invited her into the present moment.

"Is there anything to fear in this moment," I asked her. "Open your eyes and look around."

She opened her eyes, looked around, and could see that there was nothing to fear.

"Are you alone in this moment?" I asked her.

She gazed directly into my eyes and became more present.

"No," she replied with a faint smile. "You are here."

"As long as you try to escape from the fear or the feeling of loneliness," I said, "you will continue your quest to find someone to be here for you. This will never happen, because it is inconsistent with your basic belief that you are alone. You cannot win."

"What can I do?" she asked quietly. "I really want to be free of all of this."

"You are doing it!" I said. "Just feel the pain and the fear and remain present as you do so. Eventually, you will come to realize that the pain and the fear and the loneliness are from the past and have nothing to do with the present moment. Running from these feelings all your life has been nothing but a bad habit, which has kept you locked in a past that is no longer here."

She seemed to understand what I had shared with her. She noticeably relaxed.

"What are you experiencing in *this* moment?" I asked her.

"Actually, I am feeling very peaceful and still," she replied.

"That is because you are present," I told her. And when you are present, all the pain and limiting beliefs from the past disappear."

By the end of the session, she was in a much more peaceful state and appeared grateful for the guidance she had received.

Prenatal programming of the mind

Sometimes these painful and limiting experiences originate before birth. Presence makes it possible for memories to surface from this depth.

I was once working with someone who shared with me that he had always lived with a certain level of fear. He felt that something terrible was about to happen that would threaten his survival. He also reported that he had difficulty trusting women, which affected his capacity to enter into healthy and fulfilling relationships.

He was a medical doctor by profession and was a very sincere and likeable person.

After working with him for several sessions, a very deep and disturbing memory surfaced into consciousness. He recalled that when he was a fetus in his mother's womb, his mother attempted to abort him with a sharp instrument. The memory of that event brought with it great fear and panic as it arose.

I encouraged him to feel the feelings fully. He wept. He wailed. He cowered in fear and after a while he began to relax. He felt deeply relieved.

The retrieval of this terrifying event cast a great deal of light onto the circumstances of his life. It explained his lack of trust, particularly in women. It explained the vague and subtle feeling of fear and insecurity which he had experienced all of his life.

With this new information, he was able to make new choices and decisions in his life which were not based unconsciously on this traumatic fetal experience.

ANOTHER EXAMPLE OF PRENATAL PROGRAMMING

I was working with a woman who was sharing with me that she always felt cramped and often had the feeling that there was not enough space for her.

It affected every aspect of her life. She was not comfortable at home or at work. She often felt claustrophobic. She also described a deep and persistent fear that there would not be enough food for her and so she tended to hoard food.

These disturbing feelings were really interfering with her enjoyment of life.

I spent about two sessions with her exploring the feelings and trying to uncover the source of her discomfort. We were not making very much progress, when suddenly it occurred to me.

"Were you a twin?" I asked.

"Yes!" she replied. "How did you know that?"

"Were you first or second out of the womb?"

She replied that she was second.

"Who was larger at birth?"

"My brother was much larger than me," she answered. Her eyes were growing wide with amazement as she made the connection.

Her experience in the womb was cramped and she did not have enough space. Her twin brother had received most of the nourishment, leaving her undernourished.

These experiences in the womb had left an imprint that clearly affected her daily experience of life.

I guided her into the heart of the experience. She felt anger, and then hurt, and then need, expressing each fully. She then began to laugh. Suddenly everything made sense as the law of cause and effect began to illuminate all the dysfunctional aspects of her life.

CONSCIOUS AND RESPONSIBLE EXPRESSION

When we repress emotions, because they are too painful or overwhelming, they function within us at an unconscious level and cause all sorts of damage.

Just because these memories are repressed does not mean that they cease to exist. In fact, it is the repression and denial of the memories and feelings that gives them their power.

If a healing is to occur, we will have to change our attitude towards those painful memories and feelings from the past. We will have to allow them to surface into conscious and responsible expression.

THE SCREAM

Sometimes these old memories can be very traumatic. I was in New York several years ago conducting a seminar at the Marriott Hotel. There were about fifty people in attendance. About half had attended earlier seminars with me and about half were new to my work.

In those days, I would begin by asking if anyone in the group would like to share briefly why they were attending the seminar and what they hoped to gain from it.

One woman in the group spoke up.

"I live with a lot of tension and fear," she said.

"Are you feeling tense right now?" I asked her.

She said that she was, and so I suggested that she close her eyes and feel where the tension was in her body.

Normally, I would guide her into the center of the tension, which would lead to a release of it. I had done this many times before and it had always been effective, often leading to a deep healing in a very simple way.

"I can't close my eyes," she replied. "If I do, I will scream!"

Following the simple principle that whatever is arising in the present moment needs to be accepted and allowed expression, I encouraged her to close her eyes and feel the tension anyway.

"Just be present with the feeling of tension," I told her. "And if you scream, you scream!"

"No! You don't understand," she protested. "I will really scream!"

"So scream," I replied calmly.

She closed her eyes and immediately *it* began.

I did not know that anyone could scream like that. It was loud beyond imagining and penetrated every fiber of my Being. It reminded me of the Edvard Munch painting entitled, *The Scream.*

This was a scream from Hell and it showed no sign of abating. She was completely lost in the scream. It must have reverberated right through the entire hotel.

Many things flashed through my mind. I was concerned for guests in the hotel. I was concerned for the other participants in the group, particularly those who were new to my work.

I picked up my chair and dragged it in front of her. I was shaking. She was totally immersed in the scream. I called to her.

I tried to attract her attention, but she would not respond. I could find no way to get her out of the scream. And so I joined her there.

I began screaming myself. I almost managed to match the intensity of her scream. Eventually she opened her eyes to see who was screaming. I immediately got her to look around at the people in the group and connect with everyone there. I wanted her as present as possible.

When I felt that she was fairly present, I told her to close her eyes, and she went back into the scream. It was just as intense as before. Once again, I drew her out of the scream and helped her to reconnect with everyone in the group.

I repeated this process until she could be inside the scream with less intensity. Her eyes were closed. I encouraged her to look around.

"Where are you? What is happening to you?" I asked, trying to bring conscious awareness to the source of the scream.

She began sobbing deeply and uncontrollably and would shift between screaming and sobbing. This went on for about ten minutes. I encouraged her to identify where she was and what was happening to her.

After a while, she was able to communicate with me. It became clear that she was in Nazi Germany in one of the concentration camps. She described the buildings. She described the people. She described the guards in perfect detail.

She looked to be about forty-five years old, so I assumed that a past life memory was surfacing. I was able to reassure her that what she was experiencing was not happening now.

I urged her to feel all the feelings fully. She eventually relaxed. The screaming ended, the sobbing subsided. She was becoming calm.

I asked her to open her eyes. Once again, I guided her into a deep level of Presence and asked her to look directly into the eyes of each person in the group.

As she did so, a tremendous sense of love permeated the room. It felt like God was with us. The scream, which she had carried with her all her life, had been released. She was now filled with love and the light of God. It was one of the most sacred moments in my life and everyone in the room felt it. I had the sense that this healing would impact at a collective level.

That process took most of the morning. It was almost lunchtime and so I suggested we break for lunch. We made our way to the hotel restaurant, getting some rather nervous glances from hotel guests as we walked along the passageway. The woman who had screamed was seated next to me in the restaurant. At some stage during lunch, she turned to me.

"You are a very strange fellow!" she said.

"What do you mean?" I asked with genuine surprise.

"Well, you kept talking about past lives when I was in that memory."

"Yes!" I replied. "That is what it was."

"No, it wasn't!" she protested. "I was there in this lifetime. I was just a baby. It actually happened."

"How old are you?" I asked.

"I am fifty-seven," she said. "I was there!"

I ate the rest of my lunch in silence.

AN EXTREME EXAMPLE

I have included the story of *The Scream* as an extreme example of emotional release. Can you imagine what it must have been like to live with that scream repressed within you? Very few of us will ever have to deal with such intensity of feeling.

Even so, it only took about ninety minutes to work through all the emotions associated with that terrifying experience. The outcome was that the scream was emptied out of her and it led to a deep and lasting healing.

The truth is that we all have feelings from the past repressed within us. For most of us, it only takes a few minutes to release the feelings and complete the healing.

You can release lifetimes of repressed anger in a few minutes if you hit the right note. You can release all the hurt and pain from childhood in a few minutes if you are fully allowing and accepting of it, and if you remain present as it surfaces.

Sometimes, people tell me that they have already done years of therapy and emotional release work, and they see no point in doing more of it. My response is that, without the energy of Presence to support the whole process, it is not a true healing.

Part 5

THE EGO

*You cannot awaken
until you come into
right relationship with the ego!*

WHO IS WINNING?

If God and the ego are competing for you, and the competition is based on comparing what God can offer you and what the ego can offer you, who do you think will win? Who do you think is winning?

The ego can offer you all the knowledge and experience of the past and all the potential of the future. It can offer you hope and the promise of future fulfillment. It can even offer you the possibility of enlightenment in the future.

All God can offer you is what is actually here in the moment with you.

It is not a fair competition. Very few can see through the ego's deception. Very few can resist the false promises and temptations of the ego, and so they remain imprisoned within the mind, enslaved by the ego.

THE THRONE OF GOD

The ego was sitting on the throne of God when, one fateful day, God approached.

"Why are you sitting on my throne?" asked God.

"Because I can!" answered the ego.

"But it is not your place to sit on my throne."

"I am more powerful than you," said the ego. "I will sit wherever I choose!"

"Why do you believe that you are more powerful than me?" asked God.

"Because I have been sitting on your throne from the beginning of time and I have gained dominance over the minds of men. If you were more powerful than me, you would not have allowed it. You would have removed me."

"My essential nature is to allow," said God. "If you want to sit on my throne, you are allowed. You have no power beyond that."

THE EGO EXISTS WITHIN THOUGHT

Your ego exists within thought. Thought is its very structure. The more fixed your thought, the more rigid your ego.

THE EGO

The ego is you from the past insisting that it is you now.

THE EGO GOES WITH YOU

The ego goes with you all the way on this journey of awakening. Even when you have experienced the deepest levels of Presence, the ego is waiting on the sidelines ready to claim the truth of Presence as its own.

Once the ego becomes spiritualized, you are lost. It is very difficult to find someone who can bring you back.

A SPIRITUALIZED EGO

A spiritualized ego is one that has become too involved in your spiritual life.

THE EGO IS SEEKING ENLIGHTENMENT

Although it is your soul's longing that sets you off on a path of awakening, nevertheless, the ego can become very involved in your spiritual journey.

It becomes involved for one of two reasons.

It believes that enlightenment is the only way to escape the pain and suffering, or it believes that enlightenment is the ultimate accomplishment.

The ego has ideas and concepts about enlightenment, but it does not know what enlightenment really is. It has read about the enlightenment experiences of others and covets those experiences for itself.

It is very happy for you to read spiritual books and visit spiritual teachers and acquire spiritual knowledge. It wants you to engage in intense spiritual practice. It loves to feel and appear spiritual. It loves the quest.

The ego has no clue what it really means to be present. It has no clue that its role in your life will be radically transformed as you become established in Presence. It has no clue that it disappears, at least for those moments that you are truly present.

If you happen to stumble upon the true way of awakening, which is through the doorway of the present moment, it will vigorously resist. It is not what the ego anticipated.

Enlightenment occurs as you transcend the ego and become fully present. Because the ego cannot be present, it cannot come with you. It does not want to be left behind, abandoned in eternal separation and darkness, whilst you open up into a life of truth, love, and freedom.

"All those years of meditation and spiritual practice, and I am to be left behind!" says the ego. "I don't think so."

It has become very skilled at resisting any movement into Presence. You will have to bring the ego's involvement in your spiritual quest to conscious awareness if you are to awaken.

WORKING WITH THE EGO

Somewhere along the way, I have developed the ability to dialogue with the ego. It always amazes me when the ego of another person responds to me honestly and authentically. During the past fifteen years, almost every ego I have worked with responds to me in this way.

The foundation of my ability to communicate with the ego is that I know my own ego perfectly, and I am in right relationship with it. My ego is surrendered. It would seem that other egos can feel and sense this and so they respond to me as a friend.

The other factor involved in my ability to communicate with the ego is that I have discovered that there is only one ego, and we are all individual expressions of the one ego. This means that once you know your own ego, you know all egos. It is one of the great secrets of our existence.

THE EGO'S RESISTANCE TO PRESENCE

In dialoguing with the ego over many years, I have been able to identify how and why it is so resistant to Presence.

This resistance is beautifully revealed in the following interaction I had with one of my students. Her name is Jan. One Tuesday evening in Santa Cruz, she raised her hand to share.

"I don't seem to be able to remain present for more than a few moments," she said. "Thoughts keep flooding in. I am constantly pulled into the past or future. It just doesn't stop."

"Your ego does not want you present," I said. "May I speak to your ego?"

She agreed and so I continued.

"Why do you keep this constant stream of thought running?" I asked her ego. "Why won't you allow Jan to be present?"

"I don't like it when she is present."

"Why don't you like it?"

"I am afraid. It feels like I am disappearing when she is present. It feels like I am dying."

I felt moved by the honesty of Jan's ego.

"So you involve her in thought, so that she won't be present."

"Yes!"

"What if I told you that, when she becomes present, you are not dying, nor are you disappearing in any permanent sense?"

"Then what is happening?" asked her ego. "I can feel my world dissolving as she becomes present."

"When she is present, there is no thought. There is no past and future. Your world is a world of thought. It is of the past and future. When she is present, your world disappears."

"Then what happens to me?"

"You go on hold, in much the same way that a telephone goes on hold. You are not dying, you are not disappearing. You are just going on hold. And it is only temporary."

"Where do I go when I am on hold?" asked the ego somewhat tentatively.

"You go into silence," I explained gently. "It is like having a vacation in silence. It is very peaceful and relaxing for you. And the moment she wants to participate in the world of time, thoughts will be activated and you will be restored. You have a role to play in her awakened life."

I paused for a few moments allowing the ego time to contemplate what I had shared with it.

"Does this information help you to relax? Do you feel less scared of Presence now?"

"Yes."

"Good, then will you now allow her to be present, without bringing in unnecessary thoughts to distract her?"

"Absolutely not!"

"Why not? You know that you are not dying or disappearing."

"Yes, but when she is present, I am no longer in control of her life. I can't allow that."

"Why can't you allow that?" I asked.

"I don't know," replied the ego, obviously struggling to find an answer.

"Complete this sentence," I suggested. "If I am not in control . . . "

"There will be no one to protect her," answered the ego.

"Is that what you've been doing in her life? Protecting her?"

"Yes, that's it!"

"What have you been protecting her against?"

"Hurt!"

"How might she be hurt?"

"Judgment. Criticism. Rejection," answered the ego, pausing between each word.

"How old was she when you first started to protect her?"

"Four, maybe five."

"What was she experiencing then?"

"She felt unloved."

"Was she feeling hurt and rejected?"

"Yes."

"Was it too much for her to deal with?"

"Yes!"

"Did you come in to help her?"

"Yes!"

"How did you help her?"

"I repressed all the painful feelings, so she would not have to deal with them."

"What did you do after that?"

"I took control of her life so she wouldn't have to feel the pain."

"Did you develop strategies to avoid the pain?"

"Yes."

"In taking control of her life, was it your intention to help her feel loved and accepted, and was it also your intention to help her avoid the pain?"

"Yes, exactly."

"There is a problem with your approach," I said.

"What's that?" replied the ego, somewhat defiantly.

"The pain that you are protecting her from is in her past," I explained. "It has nothing to do with the present moment. In order to continue your role as protector in her life, you have to keep her in the past where the pain is. Otherwise your role does not make any sense. You are perpetuating the pain."

The ego looked confused.

"Is there anything in this moment that indicates she needs protection?"

The ego looked around and reluctantly said no.

"Is there anyone judging or criticizing her in this moment?"

Once again the answer was no.

"Then you don't need to protect her in this moment, do you?"

"No, not in *this* moment?" the ego replied, looking for an escape.

"Well, what about this moment?" I asked. "Does she need protection in this moment?"

"No."

"What about *this* moment?"

I was willing to repeat this, moment to moment, for the rest of the evening, until Jan's ego conceded that there was nothing to fear in the present moment.

"The truth is that when she is present, she is never in need of your protection. Can you see that?"

"Yes. I see that," said the ego reluctantly.

I breathed a sigh of relief.

"Good," I said. "Now will you relax and allow her to be present?"

"No!"

I knew that there was one more obstacle to pass.

"Why not?" I asked patiently.

"What will I do?" protested the ego. "I have protected her all my life. If I allow her to be present, I will have nothing to do. There will be no purpose to my existence."

"But you will have something to do," I told the ego. "If you agree to surrender your old role as her protector, I can offer you a new role in her life, which you will enjoy so much more."

Now I had the ego's full attention.

"What would that be?" asked the ego.

"As Jan awakens into the present moment, you will be her *Assistant Life Manager*. She is an eternal Being. She needs you to function effectively in the world of time. She needs your organizational and management skills. But she no longer needs your protection, for when she is present, all the pain and limitations of the past have disappeared."

Jan's ego seemed to be quite attracted to this new job description.

"I like the sound of that!" said the ego. "When do I start?"

"I would not ask you to surrender your role as protector until she is fundamentally established in Presence. As you relax and allow her to be present, you will gradually come to trust the flowering of Presence within her. Eventually, you will feel safe enough to surrender control of her life. It will be a gentle transition."

The ego seemed satisfied with my proposal and I thanked it for its honesty. I then asked Jan how she was feeling.

"I feel very present and peaceful," she said. "Not one thought is arising."

THE EGO BEGAN AS YOUR FRIEND

The ego began its journey in your life as your friend and protector. Over time, however, its role changed from protecting you to protecting itself and its place of position and power in your life.

It is now the Custodian of the Separation. Its intention is to keep you imprisoned within the past and future world of the mind, separate from the present moment and separate from God.

You cannot defeat the ego. All you can do is come into right relationship with the ego so that it will eventually return to its role as your friend.

THE DISTINCTION BETWEEN AWAKENED PRESENCE AND EGO

When you are fully present with what is actually here in the moment with you, and your mind is silent, then you are awake in Presence. Everything else is your ego. There are no exceptions.

Any aspect of you that exists outside of this moment is your ego. Any thought you have is the ego thinking. Any opinion or belief you hold is held by the ego. All judgment arises from the ego. Anything you like or dislike is the ego liking or disliking. It is all ego.

I am not saying that there is something wrong with your ego. I am not saying that it is bad or evil or that you should get rid of it. I am simply revealing the difference between awakened Presence and ego.

If you do not know the difference, then how will you know when you are present, and how will you deepen into Presence? How will you ever awaken?

EGO CANNOT LIVE THE TRUTH OF PRESENCE

We have gone terribly astray because we have tried to make the ego live the truth of Presence. It is unfair to ask that of the ego. It is a complete violation of the ego to try to make it what it is not. It puts too much pressure on the ego. It forces it into failure and shame. It feels judged and condemned. It feels inadequate and insignificant. And then, in desperation, it rebels.

If you judge the ego or reject it in any way, then it will take you over. It will control you. It will assume power over you. It will claim you as its own.

THE EGO WILL NOT RELEASE YOU EASILY

You must be fundamentally grounded in Presence and in right relationship with the ego before it will surrender its resistance and release you into the present moment.

THE EGO WILL TEST YOU

The ego will not surrender if you are only present for a few moments here and there. Why should it? It needs to feel safe. It needs to know that it can depend on Presence before it will surrender control. It needs to be certain that you are the true Master and it will test you.

The ego's test is a simple one. It knows that the true Master is loving, accepting, and allowing. It knows that the true Master is utterly without judgment. And so the test is one of judgment. It will do whatever it can to involve you in the energy of judgment.

If you judge yourself or another in any way, you are not the true Master. If you judge the ego or you are trying to get rid of it, you are not the true Master. If you judge any aspect of your life, however painful or unpleasant, you are not the true Master. The ego will not surrender. You have not passed its test.

The problem is that most of us are hopelessly lost in judgment. Judgment is an inherent part of our unconscious life.

PASSING THE TEST

To pass the ego's test, you will have to transcend judgment. The only way to transcend judgment is to bring it into the full light of consciousness. You will have to own, acknowledge, and confess the energy of judgment each time it arises within you, and you will have to do so without any judgment. Only then will the ego know that you are the true Master.

And who is the true Master? It is you, fully established in the moment of Now.

COMPASSION FOR THE EGO

The ego is worthy of compassion. It has not been an easy role taking care of you in a world of separation. Nor has it been easy for the ego to release you into the present moment, knowing that it will be left behind.

In the early stages of awakening, the ego feels betrayed by you. It feels like it is being abandoned into eternal damnation, whilst you are delivered into Oneness with God.

This seems unfair to the ego. It has been your protector in an unconscious world. It was the one who encouraged you to pursue enlightenment. It brought you to the doorway of the present moment and now it is to be left behind!

It needs to be reassured that it is valued and appreciated, and that it has a role to play in your awakened life.

GRATITUDE FOR THE EGO

When the ego finally surrenders and releases you into Presence, it assumes a new role in your life. It is a role of loving service to the true Master, just as the true Master is in loving and devoted service to God.

Why not express gratitude for its new role in your life? Each night before you go to sleep, take a few moments to thank the ego for a job well done.

After all, you are an eternal Being. You cannot function in a world of time without the ego. Without the ego, you would not even know your name.

A FINAL WARNING

Be careful! The ego will try one last deception before it finally releases you. It is a very skilled imposter and it can easily masquerade as the one who is awake. It knows how to appear present and it knows all the right words. If you are not careful, it will deceive you.

If you think that you are enlightened or you think that you are present, you have been deceived by your ego. You have been absorbed back into the world of the mind. In the awakened state of Presence, there is no thought.

However, it is easy to release yourself from this deception. If the thought arises that you are enlightened, ask yourself, "Who is enlightened?" If the thought arises that you are present, ask yourself, "Who is present?"

The only possible answer is I AM. It is an answer that returns you to Presence. It is an answer that returns you to silence.

It is the I AM of you that is awake. It is the I AM of you that is enlightened.

Part 6

Feelings

*We think to escape our feelings.
If you want to stop thinking
and return to Presence,
then feel your feelings.*

FEEL YOUR FEELINGS

It is very important to feel your feelings. Feelings bring a quality of richness and vitality to our lives. They carry a life force within them and give us a dynamic sense of being alive.

However, there are some fundamental principles that must be understood if you are to be in right relationship with feelings.

Feelings arise in the moment. They relate to whatever is happening now. They flow through you. Once the moment has passed, then the feelings vanish. They do not linger. They are not meant to linger.

If you are on a roller coaster ride at an amusement park, the excitement that you feel as you descend is immediate. It belongs to that moment alone. The feeling of joy that arises as you behold the beauty of the sun setting over the ocean belongs to that moment alone. The feeling of love that fills your heart, as you gaze into the eyes of your beloved, belongs to that moment alone. The feeling of triumph, as you direct a perfect shot past your opponent in a game of tennis, belongs to that moment alone.

Feelings do not belong in the world of time. It is important not to take them there. If you become attached to positive feelings like joy or happiness, and you hold onto them, you interrupt their flow through you. These feelings accumulate within you as memories and, as a result, you gradually become absorbed into the world of the mind.

It is the same if you reject or repress so-called negative feelings like sadness, hurt, or anger as they arise within you.

Feelings arising in the moment do not belong to you. They belong to God and the present moment. They are simply flowing through you. Let them flow freely. Express them responsibly. You will be richly rewarded if you do so.

DO NOT THINK YOUR FEELINGS

To analyze your feelings is to think your feelings. It will take you out of the present moment and into the mind.

If there is anything you are meant to know about your feelings, it will be revealed from within the feelings as you experience them. And if nothing is revealed, then just relax and feel the feeling. There is nothing you need to know.

BEYOND THE STORY

If feelings are from the past, they will come with a story. Feel and express the feelings fully but do not get involved in the story. It is from the past. It has nothing to do with this moment.

A CONSPIRACY TO AVOID PAIN

Humanity is deeply committed to repressing painful feelings like need, hurt, sadness, and anger. The major religions do not reveal the importance of feeling these painful emotions. It is as if there is a conspiracy to avoid the pain. At the heart of all pain is the pain of living in a world of separation, where no one is truly present.

The irony is that the moment you repress the pain of living in a world of separation, you enter that world. If you refuse to feel the pain, you will remain imprisoned there.

ADDICTION

Addiction is a strategy of avoidance. It is an attempt to avoid the emotional pain repressed within you. Whether you are addicted to drugs, alcohol, sex, food, or television, the underlying motivation is avoidance of unresolved feelings of need, hurt, or anger. If you want to free yourself from addiction, you will have to feel the feelings.

PAIN

Emotional pain precedes physical pain. If you feel and experience the emotional pain, it will deliver its message to you. It will reveal to you exactly what you need to know. It will reveal where you are caught in the past and what is in need of healing or attention. It will reveal where you are out of alignment with Presence. It will reveal how you are not acting in integrity with others, or how others are not acting in integrity with you.

If you pay attention to the emotional pain and respond appropriately, there will be no need for physical pain.

But if you ignore the emotional pain and fail to respond to its message, then a certain level of *dis-ease* will gradually manifest in your physical body. This dis-ease will eventually produce physical pain. Pain is persistent. It wants to deliver its message.

A FULL SPECTRUM OF FEELINGS

In the same way that primary colors make up a rainbow, the feelings of fear, need, hurt, and anger make up the full spectrum of your feelings. All other feelings are variations on these primary feelings.

If you want to express what you are feeling to another, you will have to share the full spectrum of your feelings.

Suppose, for example, that you are angry with your husband or wife or friend, because he or she did not listen to you. To communicate effectively, you would have to own, acknowledge, and confess that you are feeling angry, but you would have to do so in a responsible way.

"I am feeling angry because I don't feel heard by you."

Then you would have to feel and confess the hurt that lies beneath the anger. The more you feel the hurt as you confess it, the more effective your communication.

"When I don't feel heard, I feel unloved. I feel uncared for. It triggers all the hurt from my childhood."

It is important to be honest and vulnerable in the sharing of hurt or sadness. If tears arise, don't try to hide them. Underneath the hurt is the feeling of need. Most of us are afraid to really share what we need.

Our needs were not met in childhood and so we learned to disconnect from them. Now we are out of touch with what we need. This results in our needs not being met, then we feel hurt and we get angry. So feel the need and express it clearly.

"I need you to listen to me when I speak. I need to feel heard. I need to feel attended to. I need to feel loved."

More than likely, your husband or wife or friend will respond with love. They will be very willing to hear you and be present with you. You are not attacking them. You are not blaming them or making them wrong. You are simply sharing your feelings, honestly and authentically.

Underneath the need is fear. It stems from childhood. If your parents did not listen or attend to you, as you needed them to, you felt alone. As a child, it was very fearful to be alone. At a subtle and unconscious level, it was perceived as a threat to your survival.

And so now, when you don't feel heard, that childhood fear projects through into the present moment. You feel alone and needy. You feel hurt and angry. All these feelings are activated in an instant and arise unconsciously within you. No longer an adult, you are reacting as a fearful, needy, hurt, and angry child.

As you express the full spectrum of your feelings, in a responsible way, you begin to disentangle from the other. The feelings dissolve. Then you can return to Presence.

The next time you feel unheard by your husband or wife or friend, you will realize that there is no need for emotional reaction. Just be present and ask for what you want.

SHARE THE JOY

There is also a full spectrum of positive feelings. Silence, peace, love, happiness, joy! Be generous in the sharing of these feelings and everyone will be uplifted by your Presence.

WHAT WE REALLY WANT

All we really want is for others to be present with us. We pursue love, acceptance, and approval as a substitute for Presence. This pursuit began in childhood when we realized that no one was truly present. Accept no substitutes. Just ask others to be present with you.

ANXIETY

If feelings like hurt, sadness, anger, and rage arise within you, and you do not allow these feelings expression, then you might experience anxiety. If the pressure builds and you continue to repress the feelings, you might experience a panic attack.

The way to alleviate anxiety and panic is to allow these deeper feelings to surface into conscious expression. You will have to feel the feelings fully and allow them their right of expression through you, but in a responsible way.

UNHEALTHY ANGER

The only unhealthy anger is anger repressed within you or anger directed towards yourself.

ANGER AND DEPRESSION

Many of us have learned to repress anger. We hold it within us and it turns inward. This often leads to a feeling of depression.

If you are depressed, ask yourself if you are angry about anything. If the answer is yes, ask who you are angry at and what you are angry about. If you want to come out of depression, you will have to feel the anger and learn how to express it in a conscious and responsible way.

ANGER AND HURT

Whenever you feel hurt, it is an indication that you are not getting what you want or you are getting what you don't want. It is the same with anger. If you are feeling hurt or angry, the following questions arise.

What are you not getting that you want? What are you getting that you don't want? Did you express what you want in a clear and loving way? Do you even know what you want? Do you allow yourself to feel the hurt or do you spontaneously become angry as a way of avoiding the hurt?

The spontaneous movement from hurt to anger is a response that we learned in early childhood, and it stays with us for most of our lives. If you want to liberate yourself, you will have to learn how to express anger authentically and responsibly. Then you will have to feel the hurt.

THE SEPARATION OF HURT AND ANGER

For most people, the feelings of hurt and anger have merged. This makes healing impossible.

When you express the anger, hurt arises. When you express the hurt, anger arises. Neither feeling is expressed in a way that leads to completion.

You have to separate these feelings. First feel and express the anger fully. When anger is complete, feel the hurt. Anger is almost always a response to hurt. If you feel the hurt, there is no need for anger.

ALLOWING ANGER ITS FULL EXPRESSION

The true expression of anger is not about catharsis. It is more like playing a violin. You have to hit the right note. You have to allow anger its voice. You have to let anger be itself.

Anger is not nice. It wants to rant and rave and blame and curse. It wants to get even. It wants to punish anyone who has hurt you, and it is not interested in punishment that fits the crime. You cannot adequately express anger without swearing and blaming. Anger is completely outrageous but you will only discover this if you allow it full expression.

Once you recognize how outrageous anger is, it is impossible to take it seriously or get lost in its story.

It is important that you do not dump your anger on anyone. Do not involve anyone else in the expression of anger. Most people react emotionally when anger is expressed towards them. Either anger generates an angry response, which can lead to violence, or others are victimized by your anger. Either way, there is no satisfactory outcome.

It is better to go to your room and, in private, express the anger towards the one with whom you are angry. Exaggerate it. Ham it up. Let anger be all that it can possibly be.

Anger has a story. Express the story, but do not believe in it. You are simply allowing the anger its right to exist and express as itself. It needs to feel accepted. If you are trying to get rid of the anger, it is a subtle form of judgment and it will not lead to completion.

Anger expressed consciously and responsibly leads to laughter.

DO NOT BE ANGRY TOWARDS YOURSELF

To be angry towards yourself is extremely unhealthy. You will have to find someone to substitute for yourself. You can be angry at your mother or father, your spouse or your children. You can be angry at your boss or your last boyfriend. It does not matter who it is, as long as it is not you.

This doesn't mean that you go up to them and involve them in the expression of anger. But you must find a way of externalizing the anger. Otherwise, it poisons you internally and leads to depression and ultimately illness.

You can even be angry towards God. At least one third of the human population is angry at God for their suffering, although it is usually at an unconscious level and rarely expressed. You can't afford to allow anger to internalize within you.

THE BODY IS A MARTYR TO THE MIND AND EGO

If you choose to repress anger, where do you think it goes? It does not disappear. It is held within your body and your body will suffer as a result. Your body has to carry all the feelings repressed within you. You would be wise to liberate it from such a burden.

THE ANGER MEDITATION

To allow anger conscious and responsible expression is just as important a meditation as sitting quietly and watching the breath.

If you are carrying a lot of repressed anger, do the anger meditation every day for at least a month. After that you can do it as the need arises. The anger meditation should last about five minutes, and it is best if you are alone in your room, where no one can hear you.

To do the anger meditation is to allow the anger repressed within you full expression. There is a foundation phrase, which will support you throughout the meditation. It is, "I am so angry!"

Now let the meditation begin. Just allow anger to express. Speak the words aloud and once you start you cannot stop. Find someone or something to be angry at and let the anger flow. If you run out of words, just come back to the foundation phrase. Keep repeating that phrase until the next stream of anger arises for expression. It is important to speak the words aloud, so that you can hear what anger is saying. It helps you to disengage from the story and remain present as the anger expresses through you.

It is not catharsis. You are not trying to get rid of the anger. You are restoring to anger its right to exist and express as itself. You must hit the right note. Find the right tone of voice. Find the perfect facial expression. Clench your fists if you want to. Beat a cushion if necessary.

It is helpful to exaggerate anger. Anger is not reasonable. It wants to curse and cuss and blame and kill. Allow it to do so. Blow up your mother or father with a hand grenade. Throw your boss into a pond full of crocodiles. Be creative in getting even.

The anger meditation is a celebration of anger. If, after a while, you begin to laugh, then you are expressing anger perfectly. Anger is outrageous. You are not meant to take it too seriously. Express it. Enjoy it. Let it playfully explode within you. Keep going until it feels complete. The responsible expression of anger will set you free.

THE EXPRESSION OF ANGER AND RAGE

Whenever I encourage you to express anger or rage, I assume that you will do so in a responsible way. Do not involve anyone else in the expression of these feelings. No one is to blame for your anger. No one can make you angry.

Anger is arising because you have a reservoir of anger repressed within you. You have to take responsibility for that. In fact, whoever triggered the anger is your friend. They bring to you the opportunity to release some of that anger. You might even consider thanking them.

HATE

Hate is cold. Hate is closed. Hate is unforgiving. Hate is anger which has become solidified. Do not project your hatred onto others for it will be reflected back to you just as your face is reflected back to you whenever you look into the mirror.

Your hatred is arising out of an old wound which has not yet healed. It is arising out of a lifetime of unfulfilled needs.

When hatred arises within you, let yourself be full of hate. Enter into hatred's world. Feel it. Own it. Express it. But do not believe in it. It is arising within you, but it is not the truth. Only love is the truth. You release the past by becoming present. Let go of blame. Surrender expectation and resentment. Ask for what you want but do not be attached to the outcome. Take responsibility for your unfulfilled needs.

Slowly, hatred will begin to dissolve within you. Anger and resentment will disappear from your life. Only love and the present moment will remain.

FEELINGS

Feelings are like a river. They are meant to flow freely within you. When you repress or deny your feelings, you have dammed the river.

You have damned yourself. Experience the feelings without thought. Allow the feelings full expression within you. Allow the feelings to flow through you. Allow the feelings to be impersonal within you.

PROJECTION

When we repress negative feelings, there is every chance that we will unconsciously project those feelings onto others. For example, suppose that you are judgmental, but you do not own or acknowledge the judgmental feelings as they arise within you. You do not want to think of yourself as judgmental and so you are in denial.

That energy of judgment is then projected onto others and you live your life convinced that others are judging you. As a result you feel hurt or angry and you have no idea that the pain you are experiencing is created by your own projections.

HELL

To live in hell is to live in a world full of your own negative projections.

DANIEL IN THE LION'S DEN

The other day I had a call from Daniel, one of my students, who is also a close friend of mine. He had just returned from a trip to Spain, and he was feeling very disturbed. He asked if he could have a private session with me as soon as possible.

The next day we met and he reported that he had been feeling very depressed, even suicidal. He also said that he had been experiencing irrational fear and that he was afraid of people.

"What are you afraid of?" I asked.

"I am afraid that they want to hurt me."

He felt very confused, because there was no obvious reason why he should feel this way. I asked him to reflect back over the past few weeks to identify if there had been any strong feeling of anger arise within him. Whenever anyone reports feeling depressed, this is the first thing I check.

He carefully considered my question.

"There was someone that I was very angry at," he said. "I was at a party in Seville one night and there was a man there who was very drunk and very intrusive. His conversation was offensive to me."

"What did you do?"

"I didn't do anything. I did not want to cause any trouble. And I was somewhat afraid of him. He was very aggressive, but in a subtle way. I was afraid that if I had said anything, he would have lost control. I could have been attacked."

"And if you had acted in a most authentic way, without fear, what would you have done?" I asked.

The answer erupted out of him.

"I would have plunged a knife right into his fucking throat."

I was quite startled by the force of Daniel's answer. It was violent. It was vicious. It was authentic. It was powerful. It was frightening.

"Wow!" I said with genuine amazement. "That is what has been bottled up within you since your encounter with that man. And because you did not express it, it turned inwards. And that level of violence repressed within you will poison you."

"But if I expressed that much rage at the time, I would be in jail for murder," he protested. "I could not allow myself to feel that level of intensity. It is too out of control."

"I am not saying that you should express it towards anyone. But you have to find an opportunity to allow that energy to express in a responsible way. You have to externalize it. Otherwise it will internalize and create intense pressure. As you strive to control this pressure, it locks up your energy, which leads to a feeling of depression."

I paused to allow him to absorb what I was saying.

"If you continue to be in denial of such intense energy, there is every possibility that it will project itself outside of you. Projection enables us to relieve the internal pressure unconsciously. And that is exactly what has happened to you. The violent energy of rage and anger repressed within you is projecting onto others. Then, without realizing it, you experience that violence and desire to kill as coming from outside of you. The outcome is that you feel paranoid."

"What can I do?" he asked.

"You have to own your violent nature. You are violent. You are a killer. If anyone hurts you or intrudes into your space, you want to annihilate them. Own it, acknowledge it, confess it, and express it, but without judgment. That is the way of liberation. When you own that this energy is in you, you will no longer project it outside of you. And when you express it fully and responsibly, you will come out of your depression."

He left the session feeling deeply relieved. We met for lunch several days later. He playfully confessed that he was a violent man, and that I should be careful not to hurt his feelings or he might kill me.

We laughed and enjoyed a pleasant lunch together.

Part 7

THE SOUL'S JOURNEY

*The past from which you
must release yourself
is not limited to this lifetime.*

A BROADER PERSPECTIVE

I don't want to complicate what is really a very simple teaching about awakening. For some of you, however, it is helpful to have a clearer understanding of the journey that you are on. It will bring all the painful and difficult experiences of your life into perspective, and reveal that your existence here on earth is profoundly purposeful.

The truth is that you are not limited to this one lifetime. Before you were conceived in your mother's womb, you existed within the realm of the soul. After you die, you will return to the realm of the soul.

THE SOUL'S JOURNEY

You are a soul on a journey over many lifetimes.

Before setting off on the journey, you existed in Oneness. You were an eternal Being. It was an existence in Paradise, not unlike the Garden of Eden. But you left Paradise. You left the Oneness and entered into a dimension of time, duality, and separation. That was the beginning of your journey as a soul.

The soul journeys across many lifetimes, acquiring a sense of identity as it goes. Each lifetime lived in physical form contributes to the soul's sense of itself in much the same way that each significant event in this lifetime contributes to your sense of yourself.

If, in an earlier incarnation, you were aggressive, controlling, and abusive, without care or regard for others, those negative personality traits and the karmic consequences of your thoughts and deeds during that lifetime, would have passed into the soul at the time of your death.

This then adds to the soul's sense of separation and its sense of unworthiness. These negative traits would also carry forward into subsequent lifetimes.

If you were hurt, abandoned, isolated, or abused emotionally, that too would add to the soul's sense of separation. If you acquired limiting and self-defeating beliefs in some earlier lifetime, those beliefs will carry forward into subsequent lifetimes, until they are brought to consciousness and released from the soul.

The whole point of the soul's journey is to purify itself of negative traits, heal past wounds and traumas, and release limiting beliefs, all of which involve the soul in the illusion of separation.

Before you incarnated in this lifetime, the soul wrote a script that would give you the best chance to accomplish its objectives. Its goal is a return to Oneness, and your life here on earth can significantly advance the soul toward its goal, or it can impede the soul in its progress.

In this way, you are an emissary of the soul.

As you heal here on earth, the soul is healed. As you release limiting beliefs, they are released from the soul. As you repent and atone for past abuses, the karmic consequence of that past abuse is released from the soul.

The more you awaken here on earth, the more the soul will awaken. The more awakened the soul, the more you will be awake here on earth. These two dimensions are interdependent.

And so, at the end of your life, when you leave your body and you are reabsorbed into the soul, you will have to face the following questions.

Have you succeeded in your journey upon behalf of the soul? Have the lessons been learned? Is the soul purified by your efforts? Or have you brought back to the soul unresolved traumas, repressed feelings, unfulfilled desires, misunderstandings, bitterness, conflict, isolation, fear, and a sense of failure?

Have you managed to free the soul from karmic debt? Or have you created even more karmic consequences, which will have to be worked out in future incarnations?

More likely than not, the soul will be required to undergo further purification. This process of birth, death, and rebirth will continue until the soul is purified and is restored into the experience of Oneness with God.

REPENTANCE

If, in a past lifetime, you were cruel or abusive, or acted in a way that led to guilt or shame, the soul will have to find its way to atonement.

In subsequent incarnations, the soul might enter into a life script that requires a high level of piety and kind and loving service as a way of atonement.

Perhaps the life script will involve extensive meditation and deep immersion in spiritual practice. Often this will not be enough. A soul that has been involved in abusing others will have to come to repentance. The more there was abuse in a past lifetime, the greater the need for repentance.

However, true repentance is not possible if the past abuse of others remains unconscious, and so the life script will include ways to bring that past abuse to consciousness.

As a way of repentance, the soul sometimes creates a life script that involves taking on the role of the abused rather than the abuser. This can lead to an understanding of the words of Jesus, when he said,

"Do unto others as you would have them do unto you."

By consciously experiencing the pain of abuse, you will no longer want to inflict that pain on others. Your repentance is true and sincere.

Only opportunities

Just as painful or traumatic events in your childhood can affect the whole of your life, so too can painful or traumatic events from earlier lifetimes affect your life.

In order to liberate yourself from a limiting past, those painful and traumatic events will have to be restored to consciousness. It is an essential part of healing, and it matters not whether the past to be restored is from childhood or from some distant past life.

In fact, a trauma that you have experienced in this lifetime may be a reflection of some deeper issue that exists at the soul level. It can provide an invaluable opportunity for the healing of the soul.

When you know that healing and completing the past releases you into the present moment and the truth of life, you will know that every problem, conflict, and difficulty in your life is, in reality, an opportunity for healing and awakening.

RECOVERING PAST LIFE MEMORIES

A number of years ago, when I lived in Australia, a woman in her early forties, named Anne, attended my group meetings. She is a mother of three children and it would be an understatement to say that her life was dysfunctional.

She was full of fear and anxiety when she first began attending my program. She was afraid to leave the house. She was afraid to drive. She was afraid of just about everything. And yet there was something very warm about her. I suspected that underneath all the fear and hurt, there was a heart of gold. As well as attending the seminars, she had two or three private sessions with me.

Her story gradually emerged. As a child, she had been sexually assaulted for many years by a family member. This created in her a sense of shame, guilt, and fear, which had a crippling effect upon her life.

The other significant event in her childhood was that when she was five years old, her grandfather shot himself in the room next to where she was playing. She had loved him dearly and felt closer to him than anyone else in the family. Only moments before he shot himself, she had been trying to hug him and he had pushed her away, irritated. She somehow connected her attempt to be close to him with his suicide and thought that she had caused it. These events created a deep feeling of guilt within her, which she lived with every day of her life.

One Thursday evening, I noticed that she was lingering behind. When everyone had left, she came up to me. She appeared desperate and very needy.

"You have to help me! You have to help me!" she repeated several times, on the verge of tears.

"What's wrong?" I asked with genuine surprise and concern.

"You have to help me," she repeated, crying. "I have been diagnosed today with an inoperable brain tumor. They say that I have only three months to live!"

I felt a tremendous pull on my energy. She seemed to be somehow transferring responsibility onto me. My answer startled me almost as much as it startled her.

"Don't you know by now," I said, "that it does not make the slightest bit of difference to me whether you live or die?"

She looked at me for a moment in disbelief and ran from the room crying.

"You are the most heartless and horrible man I have ever met," she said as she was leaving. "I will never speak to you again!"

I was somewhat disturbed when I went to bed that night and did not sleep very soundly. My response to her had seemed unnecessarily harsh and it was not until later that I realized how perfect it was.

The next morning at about eleven, she called.

"I am calling to thank you," she said.

She sounded calm and resolved.

"You have thrown me back onto myself. I can see that I will have to take responsibility for my condition if I am to survive. I would like to enroll in your December retreat."

I did a quick mental calculation.

"But that is in three months' time," I said, with some concern. "And that is when you are supposed to die. I don't know how I feel about you dying at my retreat."

She persisted and I told her that if she cleared it with her doctors and family, then she could attend.

She also asked if she could have some more private sessions with me, prior to the retreat. During these sessions, we made tremendous progress in bringing to consciousness many of the painful memories from her childhood, which had so traumatized her. She was obviously healing at an emotional level.

I guided and supported her through the expression and release of very deep feelings of hurt, rage, and anger. The fear that she had carried for most of her life was subsiding. She was beginning to feel stronger and more positive about her life. And yet the physical pain resulting from the brain tumor intensified. She was, at times, completely incapacitated as a result of the pain. The headaches often reduced her to tears. The tumor seemed to be increasing in size and the doctors said that there was very little they could do about it.

The work I had done with her was healing at many levels but it was not having any effect upon her physical condition.

In late December of that year, she attended the retreat. There were about twenty-five people in residential attendance and all of them had worked with me in the past.

It was a very powerful workshop and, on about the fourth day, I was sharing a deep healing process with the group. The purpose of the process was to bring to the surface all those repressed and denied feelings from childhood, so that they could be experienced consciously.

It was proving to be very effective. Many of the participants were reliving past hurts and allowing tears and anger to surface and be expressed fully and consciously. This is the key to emotional healing. It is also the key to physical healing, if an emotional disturbance is the root cause of the physical illness, which is often the case.

For Anne, the process of healing suddenly opened up to a new level. It was as if a door into another realm had opened and she found herself in another lifetime. It was a very powerful experience as memories and emotions surfaced.

I have a deep trust in the healing process and so I just allowed everything to occur whilst being as present with her as possible. I spoke words of encouragement and support, reassuring her that what she was experiencing was not happening now, and that it was from a past life.

She was weeping and saying over and over again that she was sorry. I was able to enter into her experience and connect with her. She explained, sobbing, that she had been in charge of a convent with about one hundred orphaned children in her care. It was reported to her that enemy invaders were approaching and that they were pillaging and raping at every opportunity. She was overcome with fear and chose to run, abandoning the children to the invaders. She was filled with guilt and remorse, which carried into the soul at the time of her death. Now her soul was burdened by guilt and remorse, which would manifest in each subsequent lifetime, until it was released.

The feelings of guilt that arose as a result of her grandfather's suicide provided the link to that earlier lifetime.

In that lifetime, the guilt was too much for her to face up to and so there was no repentance. But when Anne restored that experience to consciousness at the retreat, she was able to truly repent upon behalf of her soul. As a result, guilt was released from a very deep and unconscious level, and this had a profoundly healing effect upon her.

The energy of guilt must have been involved with her brain tumor, for when she returned to her doctors after the retreat, it had disappeared. The doctors were in disbelief.

Not only had she healed emotionally and physically, but her whole life was transformed. Whenever I return to Melbourne, she is there at the airport, waiting to pick me up. That retreat occurred over twenty years ago.

ARE PAST LIVES REAL?

In one weekend workshop, a very powerful past life experience arose for one of the members of the group. As it surfaced into conscious awareness and expression, it led to a profound healing.

However, another member of the group seemed quite troubled by what had happened. He spoke out to express his concern.

"You speak about past lives and karmic consequences," he said. "But I have never experienced a past life. As far as I am concerned there is only this lifetime. For me, your reference to past lives casts doubt upon your whole teaching, and yet I love everything else you have shared with us. It all makes so much sense. Why should I believe in past lives?"

I truly appreciated his honesty.

"Your question is perfectly valid," I told him. "And I would not have you believe one word I say. I am not suggesting that you should believe in past lives just because I speak of them, but nor should you disbelieve. At this stage, the only true position to take is one of not knowing. So far, your experience has not opened up into past life memory and so it does not concern you."

He listened carefully as I continued.

"If I wanted you to accept what I'm saying, I would be taking you into the world of belief, which would be a violation of you. I would never do that! But I can speak from my own experience, not as an attempt to persuade you, but simply to reveal the possibility of past lives and the soul's journey over many lifetimes. All I can ask of you is to remain open. To be a disbeliever is no more intelligent than being a blind believer."

In my own experience, I have worked with people who have had past-life memories spontaneously arise in the most powerful and dramatic way, and not in any way that I have induced through hypnosis, regression, or any other method.

The only past life recollections that I trust are the ones that arise spontaneously as we deepen into Presence and become more honest and authentic in our humanness. It seems to be a natural part of the healing and release of the past for some people I have worked with, but certainly not all of them.

For me, the evidence for past lives is beyond doubt, simply because of my own experience in working with people, and seeing the healing that occurs with the recovery of a traumatic past-life memory. I have also recalled several of my own past lives.

RELEASING A DISTANT PAST

Perhaps, if I give you another example of a past-life healing, it might help to open you to the possibility of past lives, without asking you to believe in it.

One time, I was working with a young woman in her early twenties, who had been attending my evening teaching sessions for about three months. She also had a number of private sessions with me. She was a very attractive and loving woman, who was normal and well-adjusted in every way. Except for one thing! She was terrified of the male penis, and she couldn't have a naked male anywhere near her. You can imagine how this affected her personal life and in particular her love life.

She attended a seven-day retreat that I was running in Northern California. During the retreat, powerful emotions began to emerge.

My response was to encourage her to feel the feelings and express them fully. I proceeded on the basis that the feelings originated from some traumatic experience in her childhood. But I wasn't getting anywhere with that approach.

It suddenly occurred to me that she was no longer in this lifetime. I asked her to keep her eyes closed, but to look around and tell me who she was, where she was, and what was happening to her. Suddenly a story emerged in the midst of all the hysteria.

She was a twelve-year-old girl living in a village in Africa and she had been abducted and carried off to sea by slave traders. She had been sexually abused whilst at sea in a terrible and violent way, and the memory of that sexual abuse was coming up very powerfully.

When she had been through the worst of that past life experience, including her death, she began to relax. She was very calm for a few minutes and then she became very excited. She began to run around the grounds of the retreat in a state of complete ecstasy. She was celebrating her liberation from the past with a tremendous sense of joy. It was an exhilarating experience for those of us who were present to witness such a powerful healing.

As a result of that healing, her sexual fear dissolved completely. Within two years she was married and now has two lovely children.

Is healing necessary?

In some spiritual approaches to awakening, it is said that healing is unnecessary. It has also been said that attending to the past keeps you in the past, and all that is necessary is to be present. Then, there is no past to heal.

That is absolutely true. If you are able to remain fundamentally present in your day-to-day life and in your relationships, then healing is unnecessary. The past is irrelevant.

But many people on a spiritual path find it difficult to be present. It is as if they are caught in an unresolved past, which will not release them.

For these people, healing *is* necessary if they are to free themselves from the world of the mind and become fully and permanently established in the awakened state of Presence.

There is no need to seek out what is in need of healing. You do not have to focus on the past. Just be present and Presence will do the work for you. Presence will bring to consciousness whatever is in need of healing.

As it surfaces for healing and completion, the past is released from you and you are released from the past, which allows you to deepen into the present moment.

THE HEALING POWER OF PRESENCE

The present moment is a doorway into the past, which makes true healing and completion possible. The healing that is available through the power of Presence is nothing short of miraculous. It is as if we are invoking the grace and power of God, not only by being fully present, but also by being utterly honest and authentic in our humanness.

THE HEADACHE

A woman attending one of my retreats complained that she'd suffered from headaches for most of her life.

"Do you have a headache now?" I asked her.

She said that she did.

"It is because you don't allow yourself to feel your feelings."

"I want to feel my feelings," she said.

I invited her to the front of the room. There was a chair on the stage next to mine and, as she settled in next to me, she closed her eyes and I guided her into a deep level of Presence.

Responding to my words, she became present with her body breathing and present with the sounds she heard in each moment.

"Now I want you to be present with the headache. It is a part of the present moment. It has a right to be here. Feel it fully. Be present with it. Say yes to it."

As she became present with the headache, feelings began to surface. She started to cry.

"Just let the tears flow," I told her. "They have a right to be here."

There was more crying! She then complained that her stomach was hurting.

Whenever we repress our feelings, there is a reasonable likelihood that those feelings will insist on getting our attention by manifesting as physical pain.

"Be present with that pain in your stomach," I suggested gently. "It has a right to be here."

The tears rolled down her cheeks. At last she spoke through her tears.

"I feel so unworthy."

"The feeling of unworthiness has a right to be here too. Feel it, be present with it."

My approach was very simple. It was to encourage her to stay fully present with whatever was presenting itself to her in each moment. She followed my guidance and went through a process of feeling all her feelings. After a while the tears began to subside. She was much calmer.

"How is your headache?" I asked her.

"Much better!" she answered, obviously a little surprised that her headache had cleared up, simply by feeling all the emotions repressed within her. "But I still feel a little discomfort behind my right eye. A small part of the headache is lingering there."

That gave me a clue that something was unfinished. Something at a deeper level was in need of healing.

"I want you to be present with whatever is left of your headache. Just feel it, as if you are attending to it."

I waited until she was present.

"Now if that little feeling of headache in the back of your eye could speak through you right now, what would it say? Let it speak through you."

The headache spoke through her.

"I don't want to be here," it said.

"Why don't you want to be here?" I asked.

She began crying hysterically.

"I don't want to see. I don't want to see."

"What don't you want to see?"

"Everybody's dying. Everyone around me is dying. I can't save them."

"What is happening to them?" I asked. "Where are they? How are they dying?"

"They're in a building and it's on fire."

She was screaming. "Oh God! Oh God!"

A past life was obviously surfacing and I encouraged her to really see what was happening and to allow all the feelings up fully.

"Oh, my God!" she cried. "I can't help them. I can't help them."

She was weeping uncontrollably, and she was filled with helplessness and remorse. I encouraged her to stay in the feelings and to see this through to its conclusion.

"Ask them to forgive you," I suggested. "Tell them how sorry you are that you could not save them."

She managed to follow my direction in the midst of all her tears. She asked for their forgiveness and expressed the deepest sorrow to those who had perished in the fire. Suddenly she became very quiet and very still. An air of peace descended upon her.

"What is happening?" I asked her. "Is it over?"

"Yes," she whispered softly.

After a few moments, I asked how her headache was.

"It's gone!" she laughed.

She was deeply relieved, and she looked quite transformed. I am always amazed at the level of healing that is available to us when we are present and we take responsibility for ourselves at every level.

"Do you want to open your eyes now?" I asked her.

She opened her eyes and proceeded to thank everyone in the audience for being present with her during her ordeal. She was laughing and then crying, but now they were tears of joy and relief. This was indeed a blessed moment.

She attended a retreat twelve months later and reported that the headache, which had been with her most of her life, had gone. It had not reappeared since that last retreat.

HEALING

I do not see healing as a psychological process. In true healing, you are being restored to your true nature. It is like peeling away the layers of an onion until your essential self is revealed. It is a return to innocence. It is a return to wholeness.

It is important to realize that in the process of healing and release, you are not trying to get rid of anything. You are not trying to analyze anything. You are not even trying to fix anything.

All that is happening is that you are allowing into consciousness all those painful emotions and memories that have been repressed by you, because they were too painful to experience fully and consciously at the time. As the feelings surface into conscious and responsible expression, the past is completed and released from you and from the soul.

When you are present, it is safe to allow all the feelings to surface, because you know that they have nothing to do with the present moment, nor are you identified with the story woven into the feelings.

But the real key to healing is to be present with the feelings as they surface. The feelings of fear, need, hurt, and anger will only resolve if they are allowed to express authentically, and if someone is truly present with them as they express. That someone is you, in Presence.

RACHEL AND THE HOLOCAUST

One Tuesday evening in New York, I had just finished sharing with the group how important it is to be honest and authentic in our humanness.

"Your gift to God is honesty," I told them. "God's gift to you is truth."

Several minutes of silence followed. I was about to move on to another topic when I noticed a hand go up rather timidly. It was Rachel, a rather thin woman in her mid-forties. She is Jewish and lives in Manhattan.

"I want to be honest," she said. "It is very difficult for me to be present. My whole life is full of fear and worry and I do not understand why."

"Would you like to come out front and sit in this chair?" I asked.

She moved slowly to the front, weaving delicately through the people sitting in chairs and backjacks in front of her. She sat there, looking very nervous and afraid. Her eyes were cast down in an attempt to avoid the audience.

"Are you feeling afraid now?" I asked.

"I am always afraid," she answered.

I sensed that something deep within her was at the root of her fear.

"I want to ask you a question."

I waited until everyone in the audience settled.

"Were you involved in the holocaust?"

A troubled look came across her face.

"Yes, I think so," she answered, as feelings began to surface from a very deep and hidden place within her. "About twenty years ago, I was at a fair and there was a fireworks display. I suddenly started screaming over and over again that the Nazis were coming and I tried to hide. I was hysterical. It was very bizarre."

She began to sob and I urged her to stay with the feelings.

"When you heard those fireworks," I said, "it triggered a memory from a more distant past. What happened? What were you remembering?"

"I don't want to know," she said. "It is too horrible."

She obviously did not want to relive this terrifying memory.

"You are constantly in fear because this horrific memory from another lifetime has been buried in the dark recesses of your unconscious mind, and it has been projecting through into this lifetime. There is a deep wound in your soul originating from that past life."

Her crying deepened.

"The only way that a healing can occur is to allow into consciousness all the feelings associated with that past-life memory."

"But I've done a lot of emotional work!" she protested.

"This is not emotional work," I said. "It is soul healing."

As I spoke, I became very present with her and all the feelings that she had been afraid of began to surface.

"Good. That's it," I said. "Let it all up!"

For the next five minutes, all the repressed feelings surfaced into consciousness. She screamed and wept as details of her experience in that past life became clear.

She was just a child. She had been taken by the Nazis and had been separated from her family. This filled her with fear. She never saw her loved ones again.

"Perfect!" I reassured her. "By allowing all the feelings into consciousness, you have released yourself from a painful past."

When feelings are too overwhelming to experience consciously, we repress them and, in doing so, we take ourselves further and further into a state of unconsciousness. When we die, those repressed feelings are absorbed into the soul and are carried forward into subsequent incarnations.

In this case, the extreme feeling of fear and terror had been absorbed into the soul at the time of death and had played a large part in Rachel's life, creating fear where there was nothing to fear.

By returning to this past event, she was able to restore the fear and terror to consciousness, which released it from the soul and also from her current life. This made it much easier for her to relax into Presence.

She expressed gratitude and returned to her seat in the audience. Everyone present in the room that night had been deeply touched by her sharing.

She continued attending the groups, and as I observed her over the next few months, the change in her was quite remarkable. She was much more present, much more empowered, and much less fearful. It really was a wonderful transformation.

NOT EVERYONE IS DEALING WITH SUCH INTENSE ISSUES

For most of us, healing of the past is fairly simple and uncomplicated, once you know the way. Most of us are not so traumatized that we have to go into past lives looking for healing and completion. This lifetime is more than enough!

TRUST

My experience is that you can always trust whatever arises in your process of healing and awakening. Whether it is pain or anger from childhood, or some traumatic event from a previous lifetime, it would simply not arise if you were not ready for it.

There is a natural timing in healing and releasing the past. You can trust that timing. Just relax, allow, and express. And remain present in the process. If nothing is arising from the past, then trust that.

THE PATH OF AWAKENING

All of your past selves are walking behind you, like a shadow. They are waiting for you to awaken fully. They are waiting for you to return home, to Oneness and to love, wisdom, silence, and compassion.

The child you once were is still with you. It is waiting to receive the unconditional love and acceptance it has always wanted which will finally heal it, calm it, and enable it to relax and surrender into the vastness of your Being.

And it is not just the child who is walking behind you. All the identities from past incarnations are still with you. The seeker, the pirate, the highwayman, the sage! Each of them applauding every step you take towards Oneness.

And should you, in this lifetime, go further along the path of awakening than ever before, then all of your past life identities go with you. Your learning is their learning. Your fulfillment is their fulfillment. Your completion is their completion. For they have been on the same journey as you. Your return home is their return home.

And they will surrender lovingly into you, for you are the true Master. You have found the way upon their behalf. They will disappear into you. The past will disappear into the present.

Part 8

THE
SOUL'S
LESSONS

You are the champion of your soul.
Learn your lessons now!

THE SOUL'S LESSONS

From the soul's perspective, it is not just healing past wounds and traumas that will advance the soul towards its own immortality. It is not just the releasing of karmic debt. There are key lessons to be learned if the soul is to be restored to Oneness.

What is the true nature of love? What is the true nature of power? What is the true nature of acceptance? What is the true nature of compassion? What is the true nature of freedom? What is true responsibility?

These are the lessons that you are here to learn upon behalf of the soul.

DUALITY'S CLASSROOM

Everything that we experience within the world of time is experienced within duality. Everything we know is known within the context of duality. How can we know hot without cold? How can we know long without short? How can we know day without night? How can we know open without closed?

If that is true, then how can we know acceptance without rejection, happiness without sadness, or joy without pain?

How can we know truth without illusion? How can we know love without the absence of love? How can we know God without the absence of God? How can we know Oneness without separation? Duality is our classroom and life is our teacher.

WRITING THE SCRIPT OF THE SOUL

If you reflect upon the key themes and events in your life, particularly those which you would label as negative, difficult, or painful, you will begin to identify some of the lessons which you have come here to learn. And you will identify what the soul is seeking to heal from the past.

If rejection has been a major theme in your life, then you must have come here to learn about acceptance. It is that simple.

The soul knows that all learning occurs within duality. It knows that in order to learn about acceptance, it will have to go through the experience of rejection and so, prior to your current incarnation, the soul writes its script very carefully.

The script is cast with you in the starring role. Your mother and your father are key supporting players in your script.

Your prospective mother has experienced a lot of rejection in her life. She is angry. She is afraid of intimacy. Your prospective father is judgmental and critical. It is clear that these two people are perfect for your script. They will provide you with ample experience of rejection, which is the only way you will be able to learn the lesson of acceptance.

With your parents carefully selected, you were conceived in your mother's womb. You come into existence in physical form. You had high hopes of learning your soul's lesson in this lifetime.

The moment you are conceived, however, you forget who you are and why you are here. You forget that your soul has written the script in perfect detail. You forget what it is that you have come here to learn.

All you know is that you are experiencing a lot of rejection and you don't like it. You are just a child.

You begin to reject these experiences of rejection. All the feelings of unfulfilled need, hurt, and anger that arise as a result of feeling rejected are repressed and accumulate within you. They are then carried into the soul at the time of your death.

When you die, you are restored to consciousness at the soul level.

You remember the lesson you were supposed to learn. You remember the detailed script that was written for you. You realize that you failed to learn your lesson and so you begin preparations to repeat the whole sorry episode.

Perhaps you have been repeating the same lesson and the same story lifetime after lifetime. A different name! A different body! Different players and different costumes, but the same script!

You would be wise to look very carefully at the story of your life. Examine the script closely. What do the circumstances of your life reveal to you? What are you here to learn? What are you here to heal? It is not too late. Life is your teacher. Learn your lessons now!

JOY AND PAIN

If you came here to learn about and experience joy, then your soul will have to create a certain amount of pain in your life. You do not have to linger in the pain. All you have to do is accept and experience the pain and it will reveal its secrets to you. Then you will be released from pain into joy.

It is the same with anger and compassion, sadness and happiness, fear and love, control and freedom. Do not become attached to the positive and do not judge or reject the negative. Just relax and accept both sides of duality. It will create balance in your life. It will deliver you into the center.

THE TRUTH OF LOVE

When you are present, you are love. It matters not who or what you love. In the same way that a candle gives off a glow of light, you give off a glow of love. When you are truly present, love is impersonal and it embraces everything that it encounters.

YOU ARE LOVE

If you love anyone or anything, it is because you are love. If you get too involved in the object of your love, you will forget who you are. You will lose yourself in the object of your love.

THE NEED TO BE LOVED

When you are lost in the mind and functioning as an ego, you are separate from the source of life. You are separate from the source of love. You are separate from God. And so you are in despair. You are afraid of being alone. You want someone to be there for you so that you will not have to feel so alone and separate. You want someone in your life to complete you and make you feel whole.

Then you find each other. You fall in love. For a while you feel whole but it does not last. It cannot last. For you cannot find wholeness outside of yourself. It is impossible. The source of love cannot be found outside of yourself. Sooner or later, love at the level of mind must fail.

You will be returned to your separation over and over again, lifetime after lifetime. Until you turn around. Until you look within. Until you remember who you are.

When you are present, you are love. You are complete and whole within yourself. It is only when you stray too far into the mind's world of illusion that you feel separate. Be careful. Be watchful. Stay in the world of the present moment. Remember who you are. You are a Being of love. You are love itself.

IMPERSONAL LOVE

Love, when you are present, is like the full moon on a cloud-less night. It shines on all without discrimination. It is soft and gentle. It bathes you in its light.

If you withhold love or if you are discriminating in the sharing of love, so that some are favored and others are ignored, then you have taken the pure love of Presence, which is your very essence, and you have given it to the mind to use.

You have taken love into the world of duality. You have invited hate to enter into your life and become love's partner.

REMEMBER WHO YOU ARE

If I am present, then I am a Being of love. If you are present, then you are a Being of love. Then why do I need you to love me? Why do you need me to love you? The need to be loved is simply an indication that you are lost in separation. Rather than pursue love in a world of illusion, return to Presence and remember who you are.

CHOOSE LOVE, NOT FEAR

Almost all the decisions and choices we make at the level of mind are motivated by fear.

Decisions motivated by fear take you further into the mind's world of illusion. Do not let fear lead you astray. Find that still and silent place within, where love abides. Know that the essence of your Being is Love. Let the still and silent voice of love be your guide.

Sharing love

Once you have awakened and accepted your aloneness, the greatest blessing is to share the love that arises within you.

Each new moment presents the richest opportunity to be loving. You can share love in the simplest of ways. Be soft and gentle. Be caring and kind. Be loving in an ordinary way, without any sense of wanting anything back. If you are present, everything you say and do will be love expressing.

Responsibility

For the most part, we live our lives in abandonment of responsibility. You are somehow responsible for others and they are responsible for you.

You have expectations of others and if those expectations are not met, you feel resentful. They are to blame. They are guilty.

Others have expectations of you and if you do not meet their expectations, they will feel resentful. You are to blame. You are guilty.

All you have to do is declare yourself not responsible for others and this heavy burden of responsibility will be lifted from you.

Why will you not do it?

It is because you cannot declare yourself free of responsibility for others, without declaring others free of responsibility for you. You would have to surrender your expectations completely, which means that no one is to blame when you don't get your way. No one is guilty when you don't get what you want. You are responsible for yourself.

THE PRICE OF FREEDOM

The price of freedom is to allow freedom. For most of us, this is too high a price to pay.

TRUE RESPONSIBILITY

There are four aspects to true responsibility. When all four are present in your life, you can say that you are being truly responsible.

First, you must be responsive. You must be able to respond spontaneously to whatever is arising in the moment. If you are hungry, eat. If you are thirsty, drink. If you hear music, dance or sing. If you see someone that you like, say hello.

Take a dog for a walk. A dog will teach you about responsiveness.

The second aspect is to take full responsibility for your emotional reactions. You are constantly reacting to people and events in your life. You feel hurt or angry or misunderstood. You feel unloved or sad and it is always someone else's fault.

Someone else is to blame. They are somehow responsible for your reactions.

Your emotional reactions are almost entirely due to your conditioning and your past experiences, and have very little to do with whatever is happening in the present moment.

The third aspect is to take responsibility for knowing what you want. Very few people really know what they want. It was taken from them in childhood as they learned to comply with what their parents wanted. They were disempowered in the process.

To live in true responsibility, you will have to return to knowing what you want.

What you want is immediate and real, arising in the moment. It has nothing to do with the future. It is only when you know what you want in the moment that you can be fulfilled.

If what you want arises in the mind, then it is a desire aimed at fulfilling something missing from the past, which you imagine will fulfill you in the future. This kind of desire takes you further into separation. It never fulfills you.

The fourth and final aspect is that you are responsible for your own awakening. In each moment, you are responsible for whether or not you are present.

To liberate yourself from the prison that is the world of the mind and awaken into the present moment is your ultimate responsibility. It is a responsibility that has to be remembered moment to moment.

CHOICE AND CONSEQUENCE

Another feature of true responsibility exists within your recognition that every choice you make leads inevitably to the consequences that follow.

A very simple example of this involves eating. If you choose to eat burgers and fries on a regular basis, the consequences are inevitable and predictable. You will gain weight.

If you choose to be consistently unkind towards your spouse, the consequences are inevitable and predictable. You will have an unhappy marriage, which will most likely end in divorce.

If you choose to repress your feelings, it could lead to depression or illness. Even if that choice was made in early childhood, it would be wise to review it.

Whatever you are experiencing in your life right now is directly attributable to a choice you made in the past. Learn how to connect the choice with the consequence and you will enter into true responsibility.

Only then will you see that you are creating your experience of life through the choices you make. Once you truly understand and accept this, you will bring consciousness to every choice. In this way, you become a master of your own life.

FREE WILL

Free will exists in our capacity to make choices that determine our experience of life. There is a fundamental choice which affects all other choices. When we recognize this fundamental choice, we will awaken.

THE FUNDAMENTAL CHOICE

A man imagined that he could speak to God.

"What is free will?" he asked.

"It is the freedom to choose," replied God.

"Why have you given us the freedom to choose?" asked the man.

"It will teach you how to be responsible," replied God.

"What does that mean?"

"It means that consequences inevitably flow from every choice you make. When you come to realize this, you will make conscious choices with awareness of the consequences. Only then will you live responsibly, knowing that your choices create your experience of life."

The man thanked God for these revelations. He was feeling truly grateful.

"But there is more," said God. "I have given you free will as a test. I am waiting to see how long it will take you to come to the most important choice of all. I have been waiting throughout all eternity and very few have managed to recognize this fundamental choice."

"What is the fundamental choice of which you speak?" the man asked earnestly.

"Which world do you choose to live in?" continued God. "Do you choose to live in the present moment, which is the truth of life, where I am the Creator? Or do you choose to live in the world of your mind, which is a world of illusion, where you are the creator? That is the fundamental choice. Which world do you choose, my beloved? For the consequences that flow from this fundamental choice are radically different depending on which choice you make."

"In what way are the consequences different?"

"The answer is simple," replied God. "One choice leads to Heaven, the other to Hell."

POWER

Humanity has been lost in false power for countless lifetimes. It is one of the key lessons we must learn if we are to awaken as a species.

At the level of mind and ego, you feel powerful when you are in a position of strength or power in relation to others.

You acquire the feeling of power when you are able to impose your will upon someone else. Now someone is a victim to your power.

But this is a very precarious form of power.

Because you have taken power into relationship, and therefore duality, you will now have to experience power in its dual state.

Sometimes you will be more powerful than others. At other times, you will be less powerful. Sometimes you will be the abuser of power. At other times, you will be abused by power.

This can occur within one lifetime or it can occur over many lifetimes. One lifetime, you are the abuser. The next lifetime, you are the abused. This will continue until you recognize that true power arises from within and it has nothing to do with anyone else.

To the extent that you are still involved in false power, you cannot awaken.

FALSE POWER

We seek false power, which is power in relation to others because, at a deep and unconscious level, we feel powerless.

PATTERNS OF CONTROL

To live in true responsibility, you will have to surrender the patterns of control that you have developed to gain power over others.

Some of us control through anger and aggression. Some control through criticism and judgment. Some control through withholding and withdrawing. Some control by being hurt or helpless.

There are many variations. Identify your patterns of control and make a commitment to going beyond them. Fear controls. Love allows.

TRUE POWER

True power is not in relationship with anyone or anything. True power is impersonal. When you are fully present, it arises from within. It is the life force that empowers your expression as an individual, living freely in the world.

True power will bring you into the fullness and vitality of life. It will fill you with the presence of God. It is a dimension of God.

One who is truly empowered would never interfere with another. One who is truly empowered would never seek to control another or impose his or her will upon another. One who is truly empowered would never judge another.

THE POWER OF ONE

Because true power arises from Oneness, there is no opposing force. Opposition can only occur within duality.

At the deepest level, true power is love and, sooner or later, all the great warriors of the world will have to realize this simple truth.

JUDGMENT

Presence, by its very nature accepts, allows, and includes. If you are involved in judgment, you cannot be present, for the simple reason that in Presence, there is no judgment.

The energy of judgment will instantly remove you from Presence. It will take you into separation and, as long as you continue to judge, you will remain in separation.

Transcending judgment is one of the primary keys to awakening. But how do you free yourself from judgment?

If you reject judgment or try to get rid of it, it will thrive within you. You will have to own, acknowledge, confess, and express the judgment each time it arises within you. And you will have to do so without any judgment!

Each time judgment arises within you, just acknowledge it. Do not be afraid of it. Do not judge it. Confess it to someone who is present, or confess it to God, who exists at the very heart of silence within you.

"God, did you see that? Judgment is arising. I confess it before you, God. And I know that you do not judge me for it, for you are absolutely without judgment."

It is important to own the energy of judgment. Confess it, but do not believe in it.

It helps to exaggerate. Spend a week being extremely and absurdly judgmental. Walk around judging the flowers. Tell the flower that its color of yellow does not please you. Tell the trees that they are not tall enough. Tell the sky that it is not blue enough. Ham it up! Exaggerate! Have fun. Do not take yourself seriously.

Whenever you judge yourself or another, bring it to consciousness and confess it. Gradually you will expose the energy of judgment within you. And then it will lose its power over you. It will begin to dissolve, not because you are trying to get rid of it, but because you are lightheartedly embracing and accepting it.

Judgment will surrender in the face of love and acceptance.

Without judgment, there is nothing to hold you in the world of separation. Now you are free. Now you are like God. You are without judgment and you can come home to Oneness and the truth of life!

This is actually a teaching that would liberate humanity, if only humanity would listen.

CONFESSION

Confession is a very powerful alchemy. You are not confessing some sin for which you hope to be forgiven. Confession simply gives you the opportunity to confess who you have become and what you have done in your unconsciousness.

True confession must be before someone who is fully present and utterly without judgment. If you cannot find someone who is fully present and without judgment, then confess to a tree. It will not judge you. Or confess to God, who exists at the very heart of silence within you.

Confession is a way of owning all the disowned and denied aspects of yourself. What you hide, disown, judge, or repress lives its life in you unconsciously. It must all be brought to consciousness, without judgment, if you are to awaken. Confession makes that possible.

SIN

The only sin is the sin of your unconsciousness.

EMBRACING THE DARK SIDE

Many people on a spiritual path are seeking the light. They are identified with the light and are in judgment of the darker aspects of themselves. They are trying to be holy. But that is a flawed path. It results in repression and denial.

True awakening involves embracing your dark side.

It doesn't mean that you identify with it, and you certainly don't act on it. But to deny it means that it will act through you unconsciously.

BEYOND GOOD AND EVIL

The notion of good and evil exists only within a framework of duality. In truth, there is no such thing as evil.

Now this might seem to transcend all moral concepts and codes of behavior, which could lead to chaos. Without a sense of right and wrong, how can we co-exist peacefully with each other?

If we live unconsciously upon this planet, lost in the mind and functioning as egos, then moral codes of conduct are necessary. A concept of good and evil is necessary. Police and prisons are necessary. Belief in hell and damnation is necessary as a tool of coercion. We are dangerous to ourselves and each other in our unconsciousness.

But if we are fundamentally present, then moral codes of conduct become irrelevant. The Ten Commandments become obsolete.

When we are present, we live in recognition of the Oneness of all things. Our thoughts, deeds, and actions are conscious. We always act in integrity and no one is harmed.

We are love and we act lovingly in the world. We would not cut down a tree without the deepest contemplation. And we would only do so if it was absolutely necessary, and if what we replaced it with was in harmony with the natural world.

EVIL

What we have labeled as evil is, in reality, hurt or pain inflicted upon others by those who refuse to feel their own pain. It is too much to bear. Rather than feel the pain repressed within them, they pass it on to others as a strategy of avoidance.

Most people who are abusive were abused themselves. Hatred is a response to not feeling loved. How can you love another if you were never loved?

If it all remains repressed within you, then the hurt you feel at not being loved can turn into anger, and the anger can turn into hatred, and the hatred can turn into violence.

Then we judge it as evil. We condemn and punish but rarely do we look into the dark heart of evil. There we will find the deepest level of unbearable pain, and at the very heart of that pain, we will find a trembling child, desperate for love.

FROM PARENT TO CHILD

I have worked with many adults who, as children, were emotionally or physically abused by one or both parents.

As we proceed through the healing session, it becomes clear that the abusive parent was abused as a child. The feelings of fear and hurt and anger were too much to bear and were repressed at an early age. That abused child eventually grows up to become the abusive parent.

This occurs because of an unwillingness to experience the repressed feelings. Rather than allow all those painful feelings into consciousness, the abusive parent relates to his or her children in the same abusive way that their own mother or father related to them.

It is easier to assume the role of the abusive parent than to feel the pain of the abused child.

This has been going on throughout human history. As a species, we must learn how to be in right relationship with the feelings repressed within us. Otherwise this abuse will continue indefinitely.

We must learn how to feel and express our feelings in a conscious and responsible way, which does not result in harming others. It should be taught in our schools. Parents should be educated so that they will not unconsciously pass on their pain to their children.

In this way, we will gradually transform human life and society.

THE GOLDEN RULE

As you learn to take responsibility for the feelings repressed within you, you will be more conscious in your thoughts and actions.

You will be much more able to follow the golden rule. Instead of doing unto others what was done unto you, you will be conscious and awake enough to do unto others as you would have them do unto you.

AS YOU AWAKEN

As you awaken, there will be an end to separation. You will be living as an individual existing within time but grounded in the truth and reality of the present moment. As the process of awakening deepens, higher levels of the soul will enter into physical form.

The spiritual essence of your existence will flow into your life.

You will experience the Mind of God as a vast and silent stillness filled with endless light. You will experience all things in physical form as the Body of God, radiant with the Living Presence of the One True God. You will experience the pure essence of God which is Love.

As you awaken into Presence, the darkness of mind's world will gradually become illumined. You will have periods of intense illumination which will dissolve all belief in illusion. You will slowly but surely become enlightened. You will come to recognize the truth of who you are, where you have been, and what you have been doing. As you awaken, the consciousness of Presence will bring with it a gradual revelation of truth, first about yourself and your life, then about your past lives and then about the spiritual and soul levels of your existence.

RELIGION

Religion is an attempt on the part of the ego to live the truth of Presence. Christianity is that part of the collective ego seeking to live the truth of Christ. Buddhism is that part of the collective ego seeking to live the truth of Buddha. Islam is that part of the collective ego seeking to live the truth of Mohammed.

Religions must fail because the ego cannot live the truth of Presence. Only one who is awake in Presence can live the truth of Presence and the ego can never know the present moment. It will always exist within the separation.

DON'T BE A BUDDHIST

Don't be a Buddhist, be a Buddha.
Don't be a Christian. Be a Christ.

THE TEN COMMANDMENTS DISSOLVED

Did you know that in Presence the Ten Commandments dissolve? You don't need them. They are for people who are living unconsciously upon this planet. The Star Spangled Banner dissolves also. All notions of nationality which separate us have no place in Presence. Even God Save the Queen dissolves. We are all equal in Presence.

YOU ARE THE CHAMPION OF YOUR SOUL

You are the champion of your own soul. Whatever you learn here on earth, upon behalf of the soul, is never lost. Healing of past-life traumas is forever. Karmic debt repaid releases the soul from a tremendous burden. The soul's life and sense of itself can be transformed by your efforts here on earth.

You might be here to learn about the true nature of love, acceptance, and freedom. You might be here to awaken the qualities of compassion and loving kindness within you. You might be here to embrace true responsibility and release your soul from the tendency towards blame and guilt. You might be here to overcome the idea imprinted into the soul from earlier incarnations that you are a victim. You might be here to discover how and why you lose your sense of self in others. You might be here to atone for past actions or to heal past relationships.

There are many lessons we are here to learn, but there is a master lesson of which the soul itself is unaware.

Before I reveal the master lesson, I want to reveal the soul's mistake.

THE SOUL'S MISTAKE

The soul believes that, if it can perfect itself over many lifetimes, it will be restored to Oneness and the Eternal. It sees the desired outcome as being in the future. And that is the soul's mistake!

It is the same mistake that we make here on earth. We believe that we can become awakened or enlightened at some time in the future.

True awakening can never occur in the future. It can only occur in the moment of now. Whenever you are fully present, you are awake. You are enlightened. You are restored to Oneness. It cannot occur in the future. It can only occur now.

Whether it is your soul dreaming of Oneness in some future lifetime, or whether it is you dreaming of enlightenment at some time in your future, the outcome is the same. You are kept out of the present moment and the opportunity for true awakening is missed.

THE MASTER LESSON

There are many lessons to be learned over many lifetimes. But the master lesson is that Oneness and the Eternal is already here and has always been here. God is already here and has always been here. That which you seek is already here and has always been here.

It is your seeking that leads you astray. It takes you further into the mind. Lost within the mind, you are trying to find answers there, and this takes you even further into a world of illusion and separation.

You are here to remember who we are. You are here to awaken out of the illusion of separation. You are here to know and experience yourself in Oneness with God. You are here to find your way home.

The present moment is the doorway home. The present moment *is* your home. The present moment reveals Oneness. It reveals the living Presence of God in all things present. It reveals Heaven on Earth.

If you can master the art of being fully present, then you have learned the master lesson.

You will have liberated yourself from the prison that is the world of the thinking mind. You will have overcome the illusion of separation. You will be restored to Oneness.

It is a lesson that is delivered to your soul, not at the time of your death, but immediately. As you become grounded in Presence, the soul is transformed. The soul is healed. The soul is restored to Oneness.

To learn the master lesson is to be the Savior of your soul. Through your efforts, your soul will be delivered into the conscious experience of immortality. In this way, you are indeed the champion of your soul!

Part 9

GOD
&
THE
ETERNAL
DIMENSION
OF EXISTENCE

*Belief in God is an obstacle
to knowing God.*

A PERFECT WORLD

There is a world that exists within the world we know. It has existed in its perfect state from the very beginning of time. It is an invisible world waiting eternally to be discovered.

It is a world of extraordinary beauty. It is a world of wonder and amazement. It is a magical world. Timeless, eternal, and perfect!

It is a living world that reaches out and relates to you every moment. The trees, the flowers, the birds, the animals, and even the insects are all experienced as loving friends, sharing this perfect world with you.

It is a hidden world. It is hidden within the world you live in. It is God's world. It is here now. It is Heaven on Earth.

HEAVEN REVEALED ON EARTH

At the deeper levels of Presence, you will encounter the living Presence of God in all things present. At the deeper levels of Presence, Heaven on Earth is revealed.

GOD IS

God is the one. God is the one in the all. God is the silent Presence at the very heart of all things present. God exists eternally as all that is. God is eternal Is-ness. God is.

GOD IS CLOSER THAN YOU THINK

When I speak of God, I am not speaking of a God outside of you or some entity in some far distant heaven. God is much closer than that. Everything present in this moment is God. The present moment is God revealed.

KNOWING GOD

God cannot be known with the mind. At the level of mind, we create God in our image and we try to personalize God, so that we will have something we can believe in. As long as we believe in God, we will never come to know God through our own direct experience.

God is real. God is here now. But we are not. Mostly we exist within the world of the mind, which is the past and future. To know God, you will have to come to the present moment where God is.

GOD IS NOT AN ILLUSION

The world of the human thinking mind is a world of illusion. It is the only place where God does not exist, for God is not an illusion.

GOD IS BOTH CREATOR AND CREATION

God is both Creator and Creation. It is very difficult to find God as the Creator, but it is easy to find God as the Creation. Everything created is God. Everything in physical form is the body of God. Bring yourself present with the body of God, and you will begin to encounter the living Presence of God in all things present.

THE BODY OF GOD

Every mountain, every rock, and every grain of sand is the body of God. Every flower and every leaf on every tree is the body of God. The ocean and everything in it is the body of God. Every planet and every distant star in every universe is the body of God. The food you eat, the water you drink, and the air you breathe, are all of the body of God. Your own body is the body of God. Everything in physical existence is the body of God.

BELIEF IN GOD

Belief in God is an obstacle to knowing God. Belief is a function of the mind and we can only know God through direct experience. Belief is what we resort to when we do not know God.

God is everything and God is nothing

In the truth and reality of the present moment, God is everything and everything is God. There is nothing that is not God.
Even nothing is God.

Emptiness

When you are present, your mind is silent. Thoughts have
stopped. The past and future have disappeared. Your opinions
and concepts and ideas have dissolved into nothingness.

Some people experience this as a state of emptiness, which
gives rise to the feeling that something is missing. But it is not
emptiness. It is fullness. When you are present, you are full
of silence. You are full of nothing. Relax and become full of
nothing.

In silence

In the direct experience of God, we are in total silence. We are
fully immersed in the moment of NOW. All separation dissolves and only Oneness is. Only God is. Only the Eternal is.
Only Is-ness is. There are no thoughts. Just a silent knowing
that you are in God and God is in you, and that you and God
are One.

GOD IS OMNIPRESENT

God is omnipresent. For religious believers, this is a comforting concept. For mystics, who are present, it is a living reality.

GOD IS WITHIN

God exists at the very heart of silence within you. When you awaken to God within you, you will discover God in everything outside of you. Even the distinction between what is within you and what is outside of you will dissolve as you enter into Oneness with God.

THE HEART OF PAIN

On the last day of a six-day residential retreat in November 2003, Adrienne raised her hand. She had shared earlier in the retreat that she had cancer and that she did not have long to live. She was experiencing a lot of physical pain as a result of her condition.

"This has been an incredible few days for me. I feel so nurtured by everyone here. But the physical pain is overwhelming. It is preventing me from being really present. I feel strangely separate from myself and from everyone. The worst part is that I feel separate from God, and that is unbearable. I have accepted death, but I want to experience God before I die."

I invited her to the front to sit on the chair next to me. After a while, she relaxed and became quite present.

"Now just feel the pain, wherever it is in your body. Become very present with it. I am going to guide you into the very heart of the pain."

I could see that she was following my guidance and so I continued.

"I want you to go to the very center of the pain. It's like entering into the eye of the storm. Feel the pain fully and go to its center."

When I sensed that she was at the very heart of the pain, I asked her what she was experiencing.

"It is like a black hole," she answered.

"Stay very present with that black hole. Is it in front of you? Are you looking into it? Where is it?"

"It's below me," she whispered.

"I'm going to invite that black hole to arise and expand and envelop you. Just relax and remain present. Can you feel that happening right now?"

She replied that she could.

"Does this black hole seem to expand infinitely?"

"Yes."

"Is it silent and peaceful?"

"Yes."

"Is it still?"

"Yes."

"Would you best describe it as empty, or full of nothing?" I asked.

"It feels full, but there is nothing there."

"Relax into this infinite nothingness. Be present with it. Embrace it."

She relaxed and, after a while, seemed to be in a state of inner rapture. I remained silent for several minutes and then I asked her what she was experiencing.

"It feels like I'm in God's hands," she answered.

"Good, relax into that. Feel God's Presence within you."

I paused before continuing my guidance.

"Ask God if this is a moment of Oneness."

She asked the question into the silence, and nodded.

Ask God if this moment of Oneness is eternal.

Again, the answer was yes.

"Ask into the silence if God is eternally with you."

As God answered, she spoke the words aloud.

"I am always with you. I cannot leave. I am the present moment and I am everything in the present moment, including your pain. How can the present moment leave? It is not me who leaves. It is you!"

"If I stay present with the pain, will I stay connected to you?" she asked.

"Be present with what is here, including the pain, and you will always feel my Presence."

"What will I feel?"

"You will experience me as silence, peace, and love."

Eventually, Adrienne opened her eyes. She was quite radiant as she looked around the room.

"What are you feeling in this moment?" I asked her.

"I feel wonderful," she said. "I didn't know that connecting with God was so simple. Thank you so much."

"Good. Are you feeling any physical pain in this moment?"

"No," she replied. "I am just feeling love."

ONENESS

At the deepest level of Presence, there is no separation. There is no individuality. Prayer to God is meaningless. Who is there to pray? Who is there to pray to? There is only Oneness!

But you will not always exist at this level of Presence and Oneness. When you are functioning as an individual within the world of time, then you have the opportunity to experience your Self and to experience God. That is a blessing. Be immensely grateful.

TRUE PRAYER

To be present is to be in a state of true prayer.

GRATITUDE

More than anything else, God responds to the energy of gratitude.

LOVING GOD

Some people find it difficult to express their love for God. In fact, they are angry with God. They blame God for the pain they have experienced. They blame God for their suffering or the suffering of their loved ones. How could a loving God allow such suffering?

And so they have turned away from God. They have closed off that part of their hearts involved in loving God. This is usually experienced at an unconscious level and often originates in some distant past life.

To close off to God is to close off to the present moment, for the present moment is God revealed. Those who have closed off to God have been taken further into the illusion of separation and further into the heart of darkness. Their relationship with God has been damaged and needs to be healed.

These wounds and feelings from the past must be brought to consciousness. The feelings of hatred and rage towards God must be expressed and confessed. God will not judge you or reject you. God will love you for it. It will return you to your love for God. It will heal your heart.

COMMUNION WITH GOD

Prayer, meditation, chanting, singing, dancing, and drumming are all wonderful ways to free yourself from the limited world of the mind, and enter into a silent and dynamic communion with God. Be creative. Find your own way of relating to God.

TEMPTATION

The ego has an infinite capacity to tempt you away from the present moment.

The ego can tempt you with the promise of future fulfillment. It can tempt you with the knowledge of things past. It can even tempt you into its world with the promise of enlightenment at some time in the future.

How can God compete with that? God's world is limited to that which is here now. God can only attract you with what is already here, not what has passed or what may come.

So who will choose the present moment? Who will be able to resist the temptations of the ego? Not many. Only a blessed few!

The quest

A man was searching for the key to happiness. One day he came upon a sage sitting by the side of the road.

"Where can I find happiness?" asked the man.

"It is here," answered the sage.

The man looked around.

"But there is nothing here," he said.

"There is nothing here," answered the sage, "because you are not here. How can you know what is here if you are not here?"

The man looked confused.

"Become fully present with the trees," said the sage. "Become fully present with the flowers and the birds and the distant mountain."

Guided by the sage, the man was able to bring himself fully present, and as he did so, everything began to change. The trees became vibrant and alive. They were full of light. They seemed eternal. The flowers exploded into all the colors of the rainbow. The song of the birds filled the man's ears. He could feel the soft caress of the breeze upon his face. And he was warmed gently by the sun. He began to feel extremely calm and peaceful. His mind was completely still. Not a single thought arose. He felt love arising within him. He felt a sense of Oneness and perfection. He was in ecstasy and bliss. And he was very, very happy.

Just then he heard a voice inside of him. It was the voice of his ego.

"Do not listen to this foolish old man!" said the voice. "What can he offer you? Just a few trees, some flowers, and the distant mountain. That is nothing. I can offer you so much more. All you have to do is think and it is yours. All you have to do is imagine and I will take you there. I can promise you all the treasures of the world. I can promise you fame and power and glory. Ask this so-called sage if he can offer you that!"

The sage shook his head.

"I can offer you all the knowledge of the past," said the voice. "Ask the sage if he can offer you that!"

The sage shook his head.

"I can promise you a better future," said the voice. "Ask the sage if he can do that!"

The sage shook his head.

"I can fix up everything that is wrong in your life. I can bring you the promise of hope. Ask the sage if he can do that!"

The sage shook his head.

The man had heard enough.

"What can you offer me?" he asked the sage.

"Only what is present in this moment."

"Is that all?" asked the man.

"Nothing more than that," said the sage.

The man thought for a while.

"No contest!" said the voice triumphantly inside the man's head. "No contest!"

"There is nothing here," said the man. "Just a few trees, some flowers, and the distant mountain."

With that the man continued on his way, in pursuit of that which his ego had promised him.

The sage watched as the man disappeared down the road.

"No contest," said the sage to the trees and the flowers and the distant mountain. "No contest."

God's test

If you choose to be present, then gradually the hidden treasures will be revealed. At first it will not seem like much. It will appear to be ordinary. There will be nothing in it for you. You cannot make use of it in any way. But that is God's test.

Will you be present even though there is nothing in it for you? Will you be present for God's sake and not for your sake? Will you be present for no other reason than it is the truth of life? Will you honor God and God's world with your Presence? Will you be here for God?

Trusting God

Trusting God is as simple as being present.

The eternal nature of God

Creation is constantly giving birth to itself. Life is the womb of death and death is the womb of life. Creation and destruction are dual aspects of God. That which is born shall die. That which dies shall be born anew. That which begins will end. And that which ends will begin again. Such is the eternal nature of God.

The eternal Now

There are not many moments. There is only one moment. It is the eternal moment of Now. Everything is occurring within the eternal Now.

In this moment, people are walking, birds are flying, leaves are falling, flowers are blooming, and it is all occurring within the eternal moment of Now.

Opening into the mystery

When you are fully present, you open into the mystery of existence. The mystery is so profound that it is beyond understanding. When you recognize this, the need to understand dissolves.

Trust in God

Every leaf falling from every tree is falling at exactly the time and in exactly the way that God planned. Watch a leaf fall. Its journey to the ground has been planned by God in perfect detail. Every movement in the wind, every change in direction, and every floating, flying, falling movement is predetermined by God in perfect detail long before the tree came into existence.

If God has such a perfect plan for the journey of a leaf from a tree, then how much more perfect is God's plan for you?

ACCEPTANCE

To trust in God means to live in total acceptance of what is. This does not mean that you live passively in the world. You live in the world with love, honesty, and integrity. You live an empowered life.

However, if things do not go your way, then you trust that whatever is happening is exactly what is meant to be happening for your highest good.

Perhaps God has a lesson for you that will later prove to be invaluable, even if you cannot see its value right now. Perhaps God has a grander plan for you than you have for yourself.

COMPETING WITH GOD

When we are lost in the mind, functioning as egos in the world, we are competing with God as the Creator. We are creating our own world of illusion, and then we are condemned to live in it.

THE WILL OF GOD

Whatever is happening in this moment is the will of God, simply because it is happening. To reject what is happening in any moment is to be against the will of God. And when you resist the will of God, you create your own suffering.

Remembering God

If you remember God and live in conscious awareness of the presence of God, then your creative efforts will be in total harmony with God's creation.

You will not be competing with God. You will not create anything that conflicts with God's creation. You will not create anything that is harmful or toxic to God's creation. You will not create anything that detracts from the natural beauty and glory of God's creation. In fact, your contribution will add to the beauty of God's world.

You are the ocean and the wave

You are both the ocean and the wave. At the deepest level of Presence, the ocean is silent, deep, infinite, and still. All sense of yourself as an individual has disappeared. There is no sense of separation and there is no expression.

But when the wave appears, you are restored to your individuality. Now you are expressing uniquely as you. Now you are the wave. You are the ocean expressing itself as the wave.

Beyond miracles

In one of my evening teaching sessions, Evan raised his hand to ask a question. He had recently moved from New York to Santa Cruz, so that he could regularly attend gatherings with me. There is a sweetness and innocence to him, which I find very endearing.

"Leonard, are you really enlightened?"

"It depends upon what you mean by enlightenment. If by enlightenment, you are referring to the fully awakened state of Presence, then that state of consciousness is always available to me. It never goes away. Indeed, I am that! If by enlightenment, you are referring to the process of allowing everything that is unconscious to surface into conscious awareness, I can tell you that I am always available to that process."

"Then you are enlightened!"

"I cannot answer your question, Evan. When I am truly awake, I am fully present. I exist in Oneness. There is no thinking mind. There is no internal commentator. I am just here and my mind is silent. There is no split between the observer and the observed. So who is there to assess or define? I am in a state of Oneness and Is-ness. Others might regard me in that moment as enlightened but I cannot, simply because there is no longer a split in my consciousness."

Evan seemed to relax into Presence, but then I saw another question arise within his mind.

"Can you perform miracles?" he asked.

"I have no interest in that," I replied. "Jesus performed miracles. Did anyone actually awaken because of those miracles? I doubt it! The greatest miracle is to be fully awake in the present moment, experiencing the truth of life. Miracles are for believers, who will not believe without miracles to support their beliefs. Those who know God and the truth from their own experience have no need of miracles. *Life* is the miracle. This moment is the miracle. That is enough for me."

INNOCENCE

One who is innocent is one who is willing to dwell in a state of not knowing. A mystic is one who allows existence to remain a mystery.

IS THIS MOMENT ENOUGH?

A man was very present one day, when he heard God speak to him.

"Is this moment enough?" asked God.

"Yes, of course!" replied the man.

"Good," said God. "Then you may stay."

"What would have happened if I had answered no?" asked the man.

"Then you could not remain here. You would have to leave the present moment in search of more."

"But where would I go?"

"The only place you can go is into the world of your mind."

"What will I find there?" asked the man.

"Only empty memories and false promises," replied God. "And a future that never arrives!"

WHAT IS GOD TO DO?

If God cannot wake us up, God will have to shake us up! It is time to awaken.

DIALOGUE WITH GOD

A man was truly seeking God.

"I love you," he cried. "But I do not know how to find you!"

"Be still," replied God. "Be silent. Be present. Look and you will see me. Listen and you will hear me, for I am everywhere. At first it will be difficult, for I am invisible. I am hidden. And I speak very softly. You must become silent if you are to hear me. You must become still if you are to see me. You must become vulnerable and sensitive if you are to feel me. You must become innocent if you are to know me. Surrender all your beliefs about me, for I am beyond belief. Do not try to imagine me, for I am real and cannot be imagined. Do not create me in your image, for I am beyond all imagery. Be sincere and you will find me, for I am Love and I am with you always. You cannot comprehend what I am like. So don't try. Just be present, be still, and behold. I am here."

GOD SPEAKS

"I am the One in the All. I am everything and I am nothing. I am the beginning and the end. I am eternal silence. I am peace everlasting. I am that I am. In me, the truth shall be known. Through me, all will be revealed. I am at the very center of your Being. I am your foundation. I am your rock. Upon me, you may build your Jerusalem."

Part 10

LIVING IN THE WORLD OF TIME

Once you have awakened,
how will you live in a world
where very few are awake?

Two worlds

There are two worlds, the world of Now and the world of time. Many people are afraid to awaken. They believe that if they awaken fully they will no longer be able to function in the world of time.

There is a certain level of Presence where this is true. It is possible to be so fully present that time disappears. There is absolutely no sense of life outside of this moment. There is no sense of yourself outside of this moment. It is an experience of Heaven on Earth, which is exquisite beyond imagining.

This is a most exalted state of consciousness. You are fully immersed in the moment of Now, experiencing Oneness and the Eternal. You are immersed in the mystery of existence. It is profoundly blissful and you feel intoxicated with love.

But at this level of consciousness, it is impossible to live in the world of time, because there is no time. Life as you have known it has disappeared. There is no way to engage in anything outside of the moment.

And so I recommend a softer version of enlightenment, one which allows for the world of time to co-exist gently with the timeless world of Now.

There is no reason why you cannot bring these two worlds into balance and harmony. You must master the art of moving easily between the timeless world of Now and the world of time, but in such a way that you never really disconnect from the present moment.

PRESENCE ENHANCES YOUR LIFE

Presence does not take away your life within the world of time. It enhances it. Presence does not mean that you can no longer think. It means that you think more clearly.

SETTING THE INTENTION TO AWAKEN

As a part of the awakening process, you must set the right intention. Intend to be present many times each day, so that eventually, the present moment will become the very ground and field of your existence. Unless being present is the first priority in your life, you cannot awaken.

Your second intention is that when you do play within the world of time, which takes you into the mind, with all its story lines, thoughts, ideas, concepts, opinions, and beliefs, you will not become identified with it. You will not believe in any of it as the truth. The past is gone. The future will never arrive. You know that only this moment is the truth of life.

I do not mean to imply that life at the level of mind should cease. That is not possible or desirable. What is possible, however, is that we become so awake and deeply grounded in the present moment that we never lose our connection with the truth of life, even when we do venture into the world of the mind.

The third intention that must be embraced deeply is to bring conscious awareness to how and when you are pulled out of Presence. This will lead to mastery of the mind and ego.

The fourth intention in this process of awakening is the intention to live as an expression of love and truth, even when you are functioning within the world of time. No longer functioning as an ego living in a world of separation, you now exist and express yourself in perfect alignment with the impersonal and eternal dimension of your self.

The fifth intention is to master the art of balance as you live in a world of duality within the world of time. This can be accomplished by transcending judgment.

IN THE PRESENT MOMENT, THERE ARE NO PROBLEMS

In the present moment, there are no problems. There are only situations in which to respond.

When you are present, you are free of limitations from the past and so your response is always appropriate, uncomplicated, and effective.

Even if your car is stalled at a railway crossing and the train is approaching, you do not have a problem. You have a present moment situation to respond to.

AN AWAKENED LIFE

One who is awake or enlightened lives predominantly in the present moment. The present moment is always recognized as the truth of life, even when entering into the mind and functioning within the world of time.

An enlightened person lives in a state of love and acceptance. The illusion of separation has dissolved. He or she lives with a strong sense of the Oneness of all things.

An enlightened person lives without judgment, fear, and desire. There is a continuing awareness of the impersonal or eternal dimension of existence.

He or she is compassionate and always acts with integrity. It is impossible to be dishonest.

One who is truly enlightened sees all others as equal. This extends to animals and the world of nature. It is impossible for an enlightened person to intentionally harm another.

Beyond change

In the midst of constant change, an enlightened person knows himself or herself as the One who never changes.

Abundance

The present moment is always presenting you with infinite treasures which will fill you with delight.

Be present with the sun setting over a distant mountain or a bird soaring into a cloudless sky. Be present with the waves lapping against the shore, a river flowing, a flower blooming.

Be present with the gentle glow of a full moon upon the ocean. Be present with a child laughing, a leaf falling, a bird singing. Be present with thunder and lightning.

If your focus is on the abundance of God's natural world, then every aspect of your life will be full and abundant.

EXPRESS YOURSELF

When you are fully present, there is no expression. You are perfectly silent and immersed in the moment of Now. It is a state of Is-ness. You have transcended your individuality.

Your individuality arises in your expression. It is in your expression that you are revealed as unique.

THE PURSUIT OF EXCELLENCE

It is far better to be motivated by the pursuit of excellence than the pursuit of success.

THE PURPOSE OF LIFE

The sole purpose in being here is to be here. There might be a secondary purpose to your life, but without Presence awake in you, it is of little value.

LET LIFE BE YOUR TEACHER

Every person you meet, and every event in your life, may have something to reveal to you which will assist you on your journey of awakening.

YOU DON'T HAVE TO BE PRESENT ALL THE TIME

You don't have to be present all the time to live an awakened life. As long as you are grounded in the reality of the present moment, it is perfectly appropriate and safe to enter the mind and the world of time.

You have to fill out tax returns. You have to remember the next appointment with the dentist. Without the mind, you would be unable to perform the simplest of tasks. You would not even know your name.

As long as you know that the truth of life exists solely in the present moment, you are free to enter into the illusory world of the mind at will.

I would suggest, however, that you restrict each journey into the mind to a maximum duration of two hours. After two hours, come back and spend a minute or two in Presence. It will help you stay connected to the present moment, particularly in the early stages of awakening.

When you are at work, of course, you will have to think. But every now and then, take a break from thinking. Bring yourself present with the plant standing patiently in the corner. Become present with the pen lying on the desk in front of you. Become present with the sound of voices emanating from the next office.

Entering into the mind is a journey into illusion. It is wise to stay connected with home base. Otherwise you might get lost. You might not be able to find your way home.

REMAINING CONSCIOUS IN AN UNCONSCIOUS WORLD

As you awaken, you will have to assume responsibility for your life within the world of time. You have to work or do whatever is necessary to earn money and provide for your needs.

How do you accomplish this without becoming lost in the mind? How do you remain present in a world where almost everyone is focused in the past and future? How do you live in a world of fear and desire when you are no longer ruled by fear and desire, and when you are no longer seduced by the promise of future fulfillment?

As long as you are not driven by ego desires or fears, the quality of Presence will not be lost.

Do not compare yourself with others. Surrender patterns of judgment, control, and manipulation. Do not follow the urges, cravings, and habits of your ego. It may take a little time to overcome habitual patterns but, if your commitment is sincere, it is not difficult.

Choose to be in the present moment as much as possible. Only enter into thought with conscious intention. Surrender the will of your ego to a higher dimension of your Being and honor the present moment as the truth of life. Be present. Be responsive. Be authentic. Feel your feelings. Know what you want, moment to moment. It will deliver you through life, constantly renewing you from one moment to the next.

Do not be afraid to live at a more superficial level of Presence in order to function in the world of time. That which is real cannot be lost. It is all a question of balance. As long as the awakened state of Presence is the foundation of your life, you will not go astray.

LIVING AN EMPOWERED LIFE

You live an empowered life when you know what you want, you know what you don't want, and you can express both clearly and lovingly without attachment to the outcome.

Of course you can compromise, but do not go so far that you are no longer true to yourself.

Your ultimate power lies in the fact that you can leave any situation that is not to your liking. You can leave for a few minutes, you can leave for a few hours, or you can leave for good. This means that you never have to be a victim again.

What do you want?

God was sitting quietly one day, allowing many people the opportunity to approach. The first was a man in his early twenties.

"What do you want?" asked God.

"I don't know," replied the man.

"Then I cannot give you what you want," said God. "Come back when you know."

The second person to approach God was a woman in her mid-thirties.

"What do you want?" asked God.

"I want to be loved but I feel unlovable."

"I cannot bring to you that which you feel unworthy of," said God. "First heal your wounds, and when you know that you are worthy of love, I will bring love into your life."

The next person to approach was a man in his forties.

"What do you want?" asked God.

"I want to find a house in the country, so that I can live a quiet and peaceful life," said the man. "But I also want the excitement of the city."

"I cannot give you what you want if you are conflicted," said God. "Come to a true decision about where you want to live. Only then can I give you what you want."

The next to approach was a woman in her fifties.

"What do you want?" asked God.

"I want fame, money, and success," said the woman. "I want to be fabulously wealthy."

"I will bring to you what you want," said God. "But only to teach you that it will not fulfill you."

The next to approach was a man in his sixties.

"What do you want?" asked God.

"I want nothing," said the man, "for I see that I already have everything."

"Good," said God. "To you, more shall be given."

CO-CREATING WITH GOD

At the deepest levels of Presence, you do not co-create with God. You recognize that God is the only Creator and all desire or need to create is extinguished completely. You are totally immersed in Oneness and the Eternal. You are in a state of true humility and gratitude as you behold God's creation.

But when you are participating in the world of time, creative thought and expression is possible and appropriate. You can co-create with God. You can cooperate with God.

Just as God has a role to play in creating what you want, so do you.

I am reminded of an ancient teaching story. There once was a Sufi who lived a simple life wandering in the desert with his beloved camels. He was absolutely devoted to God and he trusted God completely.

One day, as darkness was approaching, he began the process of putting up his tent, as he did every evening at about that time.

He ate a simple supper of bread and lentils. He was about to tie up his camels for the night when it occurred to him that, if he really trusted God, he would not tie up the camels. He would trust that God would take care of his camels, and that they would be there in the morning waiting patiently for him to awaken from his slumber.

"I trust you completely," he told God. "Please take care of the camels."

He slept soundly that night and, in the morning, he walked through the opening of the tent to greet his beloved camels. He looked around, startled. He was overcome with fear and grief. The camels were gone.

"I don't understand!" he cried out to God. "I loved you. I trusted you completely. How can it be that my camels have gone?"

Then he heard this reply from God.

"You have the hands. You tether the camels."

Just like the Sufi in this story, you have your role to play in creating what you want in your life.

The first step is to be very clear about what you want. Be precise. Tell God what you want in perfect detail. Then do your part. Do whatever it takes to bring into your life what you want, and do so diligently and with love.

DEVOTION TO THE TEACHER

There is a tendency to project the source of truth onto another. This often happens in our relationship with the teacher, and it acts as a barrier to true awakening.

One Thursday evening, at one of my teaching sessions in Corte Madera, Laura raised her hand to speak. She is an earnest young woman who had recently attended one of my five-day residential retreats.

"I feel confused," she said. "A part of me wants to give myself over to you completely. I can feel devotion arising within me. But another part of me feels afraid. I do not trust you and I want to run from you."

"That is perfectly natural," I replied. "When someone is very present with you, it is a beautiful experience. It is the most perfect gift we can share with each other. It is appropriate that you would feel love for me. But the danger is that you will project the source of that love onto me, and that you will lose yourself in your devotion."

She confessed that she had done this with a guru she had been with several years ago.

"There are many people on this planet who happily encourage your projections and are supported by your devotion. They want you to give yourself over to them, and it is not surprising that mistrust should arise as a byproduct of your devotion."

I paused for a while to allow my words to be absorbed.

"A true teacher will not allow you to project the source of love onto him. He or she will be very skilled at reflecting the love back to you, until you recognize that the love you feel is arising within you, and that you are the source of the love. A true teacher will insist that you reclaim all your projections, both positive and negative. A true teacher will not allow you to lose yourself in devotion."

I could see that she was relaxing.

"What are you feeling in this moment?" I asked.

"I am feeling very present," she replied quietly. "And I am feeling very intense love for you."

"That is beautiful," I told her. "It is only natural that you would feel love for me if you are very present with me. Just as I feel love for you. Now turn from me and be present with these flowers."

She turned and was very present with the flowers on the table next to me.

"What are you feeling now?" I asked her.

She looked quite radiant as she responded. "I am feeling very intense love for the flowers."

"Good," I said. "And if you were to behold the distant mountain, you would feel love for that. When you are present, you are love and everything that you are present with reflects that love to you."

PEACE ON EARTH

Each of us makes up the collective. Whatever is happening at the collective level is a reflection of who we are as individuals.

If you want peace on earth, by all means march in peace rallies, write letters, become politically active. Empower yourself and others as much as possible, but first confront the darkness within yourself. When you are in denial of the darkness, it manifests unconsciously in many ways, not only in your life, but also in the world.

When you own and acknowledge the darkness within yourself, without judgment, you transform it. You transcend it. As you transcend the dualities of good and evil, and right and wrong, you awaken into Oneness. It is the only way to really make a difference and bring lasting peace into our world.

If you see yourself as being on the side of good, and your opponents on the side of evil, you are a part of a battle that can never end. There is no good without evil. They define each other. They perpetuate each other. It is a cosmic play that will continue forever. It is the very nature of duality.

When you are too involved and identified with your cause or issue, you are lost in a dream. It is far better to awaken out of the dream, than to play a good role within the dream. Your enemy is just as convinced as you as to his righteousness. Who is right? Who is wrong? It is all determined by our conditioning.

There is no right or wrong. There is only consciousness or unconsciousness. It will take many individuals to transcend duality and awaken into Oneness for it to have an effect at the collective level. There is a critical mass that must be reached. Until that critical mass is reached, do whatever you can to end cruelty, injustice, inequality, and abuse in our world, but always act from love and awakened consciousness, not from fear, hatred, or anger.

If you want to change this world, you will have to change yourself. If you want to bring an end to pain, suffering, and conflict, you will have to bring all that is dark and painful within you into the full light of consciousness.

At the very least, your own life will be transformed as you bring awareness to your ego, and confess every aspect of pain and darkness hidden within you. It will lead to a deepening into Presence and your life will be transformed.

If enough of us awaken, then the world will be redeemed.

Part 11

DEATH
AS A
PART OF LIFE

For one who is awake,
death is seen as an illusion.

Beyond death

If you master the art of being present as you live this life, then you will be able to be present as you leave this life. Then you will not know death. You will only know life and that moment of transition from one realm of existence to another, which we call death. In the present moment, there is no death. There is only life.

Death is an illusion

The only way you can know death is with your mind. You can anticipate death, which creates a fear of death, but death never arrives. It only approaches. If you relax and remain present, and you do not anticipate what is approaching, then there is only this moment and, in this moment, there is no death. There is only life.

Eternal life

At the deepest level of eternal Presence, you have always been and you will always be. This is what Jesus meant when he said,

"Before Abraham was, I am."

ACCEPTING DEATH

I've had the opportunity to face death, where I was absolutely convinced that death was imminent and that I was about to die.

I surrendered and said yes.

This marked a transitional period for me in my own journey of awakening. As it turned out, I did not die, but something opened within me in that moment of true surrender. The acceptance of death is an essential prerequisite to living life fully. It is also a prerequisite to being present, for to be present is to die to the past, moment to moment.

THE DEATH MEDITATION

For those with a high level of fear of death, I suggest the following meditation, which will bring the fear of death to consciousness and bring about acceptance and surrender.

Close your eyes and become present in your breathing body. Bring yourself present with the sounds you hear, moment to moment. Bring yourself present with the feeling of air upon your face. Bring yourself present with the feeling of space within you and all around you.

If you are truly present, you will feel silent, peaceful, and calm. After one or two minutes in Presence, say these words to God, who exists at the very heart of silence within you. Speak from silence into silence.

"Beloved God, I am ready. If it is your will that I should die, I am ready to surrender. You may take me now. I give myself over to you completely."

Remain present for the next three minutes in a state of readiness and surrender. If you do not die within three minutes, then say these words.

"Thank you, God. I accept that you have given me another twenty-four hours to be here and enjoy life fully."

Repeat this meditation every day for a month.

WHY IS DEATH SO PAINFUL?

I was working with a student, Rick, who had become a close friend of mine. Several months before our session, he received word that his mother was dying of cancer. Rushing home to Canada, he spent months watching this vibrant woman wither and die. He did not handle her passing well. Watching the long illness take its toll upon his mother was too painful to bear. The whole experience left him totally depleted.

"Why is death so painful?" he asked with a sincerity that touched me deeply.

"Death is so painful because we are attached to the life we know. We are attached to our loved ones. We are attached to people and possessions. We are even attached to the routine of our lives. Death is the end of that. And what comes after death is a journey into the unknown. Naturally, we are afraid. We are afraid for ourselves and we are afraid for our loved ones, because we are afraid of the unknown."

"How do I overcome the fear of the unknown? How do I overcome the fear of death?"

"If you knew with absolute certainty that you existed prior to your conception and that you continue after your death, you would relax. You would know that death is not just an ending. It is also a beginning. It is only when we awaken fully into the present moment that we recognize the eternal nature of our existence. It is only when we enter into complete cooperation with death that we begin to live life fully.

To be in right relationship with death, we must learn to die to the moment that has just passed. Then we are continually renewed into the present moment, and that is where life is. Death is not something to be afraid of. What is to be feared is to not live life fully."

As Rick reflected on my words something was stirring deep within him.

"What are you feeling right now?" I asked him.

"Very sad."

"Close your eyes and really feel into the sadness," I gently urged. "Don't resist it. Don't struggle against it. Let it be what it is."

He had been through this process with me before and was able to tune in to the sadness and feel it fully.

"If the feeling of sadness could speak and express itself in a single sentence, what would it say?"

"I miss you mom and I'm so sorry you had to suffer."

An overwhelming sense of loss engulfed him.

"That's it, let that come. Let it up."

The grief came pouring out, first anger and then tears.

"Would you like to speak to your mother?" I asked. "I can call her here to this session and it will give you an opportunity to complete anything with her that is incomplete."

"How can you do that?" he asked through his tears.

"It's just something that opened up following one of my awakenings. I am able to call your mother here from wherever she is on her soul's journey. It is beyond anything you can imagine. Through the power of Presence, she will actually appear in your inner vision. Do you want me to call her here?"

He nodded and so I called upon his mother to the session. His eyes were still closed.

"Can you see your mother in front of you right now?" I asked.

"Yes! I can see her very clearly. It feels like she is really here. I can almost reach out and touch her."

"What do you want to say to your mother? Speak very clearly to her and she will respond to you."

"I miss you, mom. And I feel bad that you suffered so much in the hospital."

He began to feel guilty.

"You were so brave. I wanted to help you more than I did. I wanted to make you better. I didn't even tell you how much I love you."

"How is she responding to you?" I asked.

"She is telling me about her death. She is saying that, two days before she died, she found peace and knew that there was nothing to worry about. She felt completely wrapped in a warm and beautiful love. Fully protected, she looked forward to wherever she was going."

I guided him into a deep communion with his mother. Eventually, he opened his eyes and looked at me.

"At the time of her death, I was unable to meet her in that place of peace," he explained. "I was too absorbed in my own grief. But just now Leonard, guided by you, I was able to meet her in that loving place. It is a completion I had not been able to find on my own."

"Is there anything she wants to say to you?"

"She's telling me that when she accepted God's decision that she was to leave her body, it brought her great happiness. She wants me to accept it too."

I could see that Rick was resisting.

"We are meant to live our lives surrendered to the will of God," I told him. "Whatever is happening in each moment is the will of God, simply because it is happening."

"Does this mean I have to surrender to suffering?"

"You are not surrendering to suffering. You are surrendering to what is happening in your life, even if that involves the death of a loved one. It is your refusal to accept what is happening that creates your suffering. Your mother's passing could have been a joyful event for you, if you had accepted it and joined her in the state of grace that she had entered into."

Rick seemed to understand. He relaxed and slowly settled into Presence. He continued to communicate with his mother until it felt complete.

ELLEN AND THE ANGELS OF DEATH

In New York, several years ago, a friend and student of mine, Lesley, asked me if I would offer a private session to a friend of hers, who had been quite ill. In fact, Ellen was too ill to travel and I would have to visit her at her home on Long Island.

Of course I agreed to this, and on the day of our appointment, I was driven to Ellen's house. As we approached, I was quite surprised to see that Ellen lived in a large mansion with beautifully manicured gardens. We drove up the long winding driveway and parked the car. We were greeted by a somber looking woman in a nurse's uniform.

I went to use the restroom and Lesley went to Ellen's room to announce our arrival. She had not seen Ellen for some time and wanted to connect quickly with her in private. On my way out, Lesley intercepted me with a look of concern upon her face.

"She is much worse than I realized," she informed me.

I followed Lesley into Ellen's room. Ellen was propped up on some pillows on what appeared to be a hospital bed. She had tubes running into her nose and her arm, and she was very, very pale. It looked to me like she did not have long to live.

My initial response was that I felt intrusive.

"I am really not sure how I can be of service to you," I said.

Ellen's voice was weak and shaky.

"I liked your book," she replied. "You've come all this way. Why don't you stay for a while?"

She was very sweet and I was quite moved by her innocence. Lesley left the room and the session began. I sat with her for about five minutes before speaking.

"What are you feeling?" I asked her.

She paused for a while, as if feeling inside herself.

"I am afraid. I am afraid to die," she said.

She began to cry. I took her hand and just sat with her in Presence, looking directly into her tear-filled eyes. There did not seem to be any point in denying that death was approaching.

"It is okay to feel afraid," I said. "Just feel the fear. We all die, and we are all afraid to die. And yet death is an inevitable part of life."

We looked into each other's eyes. I could see the fear within her. It was bordering on panic.

"Tell me again what you are feeling," I said gently. I wanted her to connect with the feeling. I wanted her to feel the fear and be present with it.

"I am afraid. I don't want to die."

There were more tears.

"Feel the fear," I said, encouraging her to remain present. "Just feel the fear! Don't try to get away from it."

She seemed to respond to my suggestion. After a while, the tears stopped. There was quite a long time in silence. Her eyes were closed and I remained fully present with her. At last, she spoke.

"The fear has stopped," she said with some degree of surprise. "I am feeling peaceful now."

She opened her eyes and smiled at me.

"I am feeling this deep peace. It is beautiful," she said.

She closed her eyes again and relaxed into the feeling of deep peace that was arising within her.

"This is beautiful," she softly repeated several times with her eyes still closed. Suddenly her whole face lit up with the brightest smile.

"The angels are here," she said. "There are angels here with me."

Her expression was a mixture of astonishment and delight.

"They're telling me that everything is just fine and that there's nothing to fear."

Suddenly she opened her eyes and looked directly at me.

"They're telling me that they sent you to me!"

Silently, we looked into each other's eyes. She was now very present with me. The strongest feeling of love existed between us in that eternal moment of Presence. Her whole Being was radiant with light, so much so, that I could hardly see her face. She was quite literally dissolving into light.

"You are dissolving into light," I told her.

"Am I really?" she asked, with the innocence of a child.

I nodded and she closed her eyes to feel it.

"Is it still there?" she asked with her eyes still closed. "Am I still dissolving into light?"

"Even more so," I said gently.

And it was true. Her whole body was radiant with light and there was so much light around her head that I could hardly see the physical features of her face. She relaxed and delighted in the fact that she was transforming into light.

Several minutes passed before the next revelation.

"God is with me," she said in a tone of whispered awe. "God is with me."

She was obviously in some kind of inner rapture. After a while, she opened her eyes.

"Thank you so much," she whispered. "I am ready to die now. I am not afraid."

"Are you sure?" I asked.

She nodded, and with a smile, closed her eyes in readiness to leave her body.

We still had about twenty minutes of our one-hour session to go. I sat with her in silence and Presence and we waited together for her to die. After about twenty minutes, I gently interrupted the silence.

"How are you feeling?" I asked.

She opened one eye.

"Actually, I am feeling stronger," she said. "I don't think it is going to happen today."

I told her that it was time for me to leave and asked if she would like me to return tomorrow. She said yes, and so the next day I returned at the same time. The hour passed pleasantly, without her demise. In fact, I returned for the next three days and each day she was growing stronger. As far as I know, she is still alive but I have not maintained contact with her.

My experience with Ellen was one of the most sacred experiences of my life and confirmed what I already knew. It is so important to feel and acknowledge our fears, and to remain present with our feelings in all situations, but particularly in the event of death.

THE FALL

There is something far worse than death. It's called *The Fall!*

The truth is that we are all fallen, and it is so painful and distressing that we bury it deep within our minds, and way beyond our conscious awareness. We are extremely resistant to accepting that we are fallen. It is just too painful.

And what is the fall? Let me be very clear. It is a fall in consciousness, and the whole of humanity is fallen.

The fall is from the truth of life into a world of illusion. It is a fall from Oneness into separation. It is a fall from love, truth, and power. It is a fall from grace and innocence. It is a fall from knowing. It is a fall from God.

We cannot arise and awaken unless we accept that we are fallen.

Jesus referred to those who had fallen as being dead. If you were lost in your mind, and you could not or would not respond to his call to awaken, you were dismissed by him as dead.

"Let the dead bury the dead," he told one disciple.

His invitation, to those who could respond to him, was to be resurrected into life.

Come! Redeem yourself. Leave the world of illusion behind. It is for the dead, not the living! Free yourself from the world of the mind and ego and enter fully into life through the doorway of the present moment.

It is not the meek who shall inherit the earth. It is those who awaken and arise in mastery who shall inherit the earth. It is your destiny. It is the fulfillment of your service to God. It is the completion of your soul's journey.

And when you do complete your journey, and you are fundamentally established in Presence, then you may declare,

"God, it is accomplished. At last I am at home. I am at home in the world of Now."

And the angels will sing, "Hallelujah!"

For those who are interested . . .

AWAKENINGS

In the following pages,
I describe my own process
of awakening.
My awakening was sudden,
but yours can be gradual.
Either way, we end up
in the same place.
Here! Now!

THE FIRST AWAKENING

In December of 1981, I attended a weeklong personal growth intensive at the Jasmine Retreat, at Upper Thora, a thirty minute drive from Bellengen in New South Wales, a state of Australia.

The workshop was wonderful. I participated fully in the processes and gained a great deal during those seven days.

At the end of the workshop, I went down to the river. We had swum there every day, enjoying the cool, fast-flowing water. There were some rapids in front of where I was standing, and just beyond the rapids was a deep swimming hole. On the other side of the river, the densely forested bank rose sharply upwards towards the sky.

With the sun warming my body, I stood on the bank of the river, appreciating the natural beauty of my environment.

Suddenly, I found myself being taken through a spontaneous meditation, which unfolded in stages over the next fifteen or twenty minutes. I didn't know what was happening or what I was doing. In a way, the meditation was being done to me.

Each sequence of the meditation was spontaneous and unplanned. It was as though, in some mysterious way, I was being moved from within.

I felt my arms opening and for about ten minutes, I stood with arms outstretched and became very present with the trees on the opposite bank of the river. I embraced the trees with my consciousness and became one with them.

I felt their silent splendor and their enduring strength within me.

After about ten minutes, I walked slowly into the river. The day before, it had been raining and the river was quite high. The waters before me flowed rapidly over the rocks. It was difficult to gain a foothold, but I managed to walk into the river, where the rapids were at their strongest.

The water was about chest high or perhaps a little lower. I turned to face the force of the flowing river. Under normal circumstances, there was no way that I could stand against the rapids. I would have been swept away. But I had the trees within me. I felt an incredible inner power and stability. I defied the rapids with my strength and will.

I stood against the river for about ten minutes. Then, without thinking, I took three or four strong strokes through the rapids to the deep swimming hole, which lay just beyond.

Spontaneously, I dived deeply. The swimming hole was dark and murky and I had the sense that I was diving into the very depths of darkness. As I surfaced, I let out a sound which I can only describe as a primal roar. The sound filled the whole valley as it emerged from deep within me. It seemed like a declaration that I had finally arrived. I repeated this process three times, each time emerging from the water with a primal roar.

I then took three or four strokes forward into the heart of the rapids and surrendered to the river. I let go completely and was carried downstream. My eyes were closed. I was face down. I was swept over rocks and I gave no thought to protecting myself. I could easily have been injured or knocked unconscious.

But I surrendered and trusted the river completely.

The river slowed down about a quarter of a mile downstream. As I made my way to the river bank, I could tell that I was in a completely different dimension. I was in an altered state of consciousness. It was my first experience of the awakened state, although I had no idea at that time what was happening to me.

Nothing in my life so far could have prepared me for what I experienced as I emerged from the river.

Time had disappeared. I was overwhelmed with a sense of love and Oneness. I was overwhelmed with a sense of the sacred and the divine. Everything seemed perfect to me. Everything was alight from within. I was in a state of total bliss.

Magic was in the air as I set off along the road that ran beside the river.

I had awakened into a world of extraordinary beauty and I felt completely intoxicated with divine love. I found myself saying "I love you" over and over again. I could not stop. I told the cows grazing in the meadow that I loved them. I told the trees that I loved them. I told the sky and the clouds and the river that I loved them.

Songs of love, which I had not heard before, began pouring out of me.

Everything I saw and heard was embraced by my love. I felt like Saint Francis of Assisi as I walked down that gravel road. Everything in existence was perfect. I was filled with a sense of wonder and amazement.

I walked for several hours and then decided to return to the retreat. By the time I got back it was dark. I went into one of the bedrooms where everyone from the group had gathered. I felt very vulnerable. I couldn't speak to anyone but I wanted to be with them. I sat on the bed and just watched.

Nobody spoke to me. It was as if I was not there. I felt great love for everyone, but also a sense of amazement. As I was sitting on the bed, watching them engage in friendly conversation, an extraordinary thing began to happen.

I could see that they were talking to each other. Their mouths were moving but I couldn't hear them. Somehow, the sound had been turned off and everything was moving in slow motion. I looked at their faces and could see another face behind the one they were presenting. It was as though they were wearing masks. The outer face was not their true face. Behind the happy face, I could see despair. Behind the face of laughter, I could see tears.

In those moments sitting in that room, nothing could be hidden from me. It was like I had X-ray vision. I had no judgment of these people. In fact, I felt great love and compassion for them. However, the experience was overwhelming. I had never known anything like it before. I had no idea what was happening to me.

After a little while we went over to the main house for dinner. The Jasmine Retreat was owned and operated by Ian and Robyn Towner. Several years earlier, they had felt a strong call to build the retreat, even though at the time they did not fully understand why they were doing so. They had a powerful connection with the land and the trees and the river. They had worked long and hard to create beautiful gardens, abundant with flowers and shrubs and trees.

Ian was a wonderful and mysterious man. For the past week, during the intensive, he and Robin had cared for their guests in a very loving and devoted way. I had been deeply touched by their loving service. I went up to Ian and asked him if he had something to tell me. I had suddenly felt compelled to do so.

He looked at me strangely and shook his head.

"I don't have anything to tell you," he said.

I felt puzzled and a little embarrassed. I did not know why I had asked him that question. A few minutes later he came up to me.

"I do have something to tell you," he said. "I didn't know it at the time but it just came to me. It was a very clear message."

"What is it?" I asked.

"You can't own anything," he told me.

I didn't really understand the meaning of his message, but

later it became clear. It helped me realize that whatever was happening to me was not mine to own. I was not to become personally identified with what was occurring. That message really helped to prevent my ego from becoming inflated by the experience.

During the next few days of this awakening, I was taken through a process of healing. It was revealed to me how I had been wounded emotionally as a child and all the ways I had become dysfunctional. My fears and insecurities were brought to the surface for me to see. All my character flaws and defects were shown to me very clearly, but without any judgment. All the events of my life and childhood were being restored into conscious awareness.

As this process continued, I began to feel great compassion for myself, and I opened into an even deeper level of love. The whole world was alight with love. Everything was wondrous and magical.

A song spontaneously arose within me.

"The river Jordan is deep and wide. I found my love on the other side."

I had no idea where that song was coming from. I sang these words over and over again in a strong baritone voice. It brought up feelings of rapture from deep within me.

After a while, the song subsided and I began to receive a flow of insights and revelations about the nature of the human condition. Some significant keys to spiritual awakening were being revealed. My consciousness was opening up to the wisdom of the ages. Like a waterfall cascading from some great and timeless river, truth and wisdom began to pour out of me. It was an exhilarating experience.

All of a sudden, the energy changed. The level of love dramatically intensified. I felt a Presence within me and around me that I had not known before. Even though I had been an agnostic prior to this moment, I knew that it was God. It was unmistakable. And God began to speak to me. I was asked by God to tell the truth about Jesus.

I did not know what God was talking about.

"I don't know the truth about Jesus!" I protested. "And even if I did know, I would be too afraid to speak about it publicly!"

"As you wish, my beloved," was God's reply.

In that moment of God's reply, I discovered that God was loving, accepting, and allowing beyond anything I could imagine. I was allowed to say no to God. Every now and then, God repeated the request to tell the truth about Jesus, and I continued to say no.

To my amazement, I discovered that God was completely without judgment. God was an allowing God, who filled my whole Being with an overwhelming sense of unconditional love and acceptance.

I remained in a heightened state of consciousness for about three weeks. I was in the eternal realm, in which time seemed to have no place. I saw beauty and Oneness in everything.

The day finally arrived when it was time to leave this beautiful sanctuary. I had no idea where I would go or what I would do. I couldn't even remember how to drive my car. It was as if the past had been extinguished within me.

I found the keys to the car, but I didn't know what to do with them. I waited for a while until it slowly came back to me. I inserted the key, turned the ignition on, placed my hands on the steering wheel, pressed gently on the accelerator pedal, and the car moved forward. It was a very strange feeling. I felt like I was driving for the first time and yet the skills to drive a car were fully developed within me. I knew how to drive.

I visited several friends in the area, then headed south to join a friend in Woolongong, which is about an hour's drive south of Sydney. I was still in an awakened state of consciousness, but I had come down from the peak of the experience. Eventually, I was returned to a more normal existence. It was time for integration.

Three years would pass before I experienced the second awakening. It was during this second awakening that the truth about Jesus was revealed. It was during this second awakening that I entered fully into Heaven on Earth.

THE SECOND AWAKENING

It had taken three years to integrate the experience of that first awakening. During that time, I read extensively and visited several Masters in India in an endeavor to understand what had happened to me.

Gradually, I was returned to the Oneness and love that I had experienced three years earlier, but it was much softer and I was able to function more easily in the world.

I began to run groups, sharing with others what had been revealed to me.

In December of 1984, I returned to the Jasmine Retreat Center, where I had experienced my first awakening. This time I was running the retreat. There were about thirty people in attendance, and most of them had worked with me for over a year.

It was a very powerful event and almost everyone opened into the deepest levels of awakened Presence.

On the last day of the retreat, I began to open into the eternal dimension of existence. Time had disappeared and I knew that I was entering into another peak experience. This one seemed even more powerful than the first. I experienced Oneness with everything I encountered. It was magical. It was full of mystery and wonder. I was in a state of perfect silence, Presence, and love.

I spent the next few days in blissful communion. The trees, the flowers, the birds, and even the insects were experienced as loving friends, sharing this beautiful world with me.

On about the fifth day, I lay down on the grass to rest. I closed my eyes, stretched my arms out wide, and relaxed deeply. I could hear the sound of the river in the distance. I could hear birds singing. My mind was silent, and I was in a state of perfect Presence.

Then, all of a sudden, I found myself transported through time into another dimension. Somehow, I was on the cross, experiencing the crucifixion in perfect detail. It was as though I was looking through the eyes of Jesus, hearing all the sounds and feeling all the feelings involved in that experience. I felt the physical pain of the crucifixion, and I experienced that terrible moment on the cross when he cried out, "My God, My God, why hast thou forsaken me?"

Then followed a series of revelations about what really happened to Jesus on the cross, and what has happened to him since his death.

This process of revelation unfolded over the next few days. I was in several different realms of consciousness at the same time. It was very confusing and quite a difficult experience to go through. I felt overwhelmed by these revelations. Although they affirmed the divinity of Jesus at the deepest level, nevertheless there were some startling departures from traditional Christian beliefs.

By the time this awakening began to subside, I was completely exhausted. I had not slept for many nights, nor had I eaten much.

Some close friends drove me to Byron Bay and I stayed in a cabin behind their house. I collapsed into bed and slept for three days. When I awakened, I was in Heaven on Earth.

It is difficult to describe what it was really like. I can only say that I no longer existed as an individual. I had been completely absorbed into Oneness. My mind was utterly silent. The past and future had disappeared. Quite literally, there was no life outside the present moment.

The cabin was set in a beautiful forest. It was quiet and secluded and all I could hear was the sound of birds singing. For the next three weeks, I lay in bed or sat in a chair by the window, totally immersed in the mystery of existence. Occasionally, I went for a walk, but my body was quite weakened by the experience.

I had very few visitors during this time, and the few that did come did not really know how to be with me. I was not able to engage in conversation, but if anyone asked a question or sought guidance, I could respond. I was in a constant state of profound love and Oneness.

Then one day, these words spontaneously arose from deep within me.

"No one will come."

Somehow these four words conveyed a message to me. I must come down from the mountainous heights of consciousness and return to a more normal level. Then I could function in the world of time and make myself available to others seeking guidance.

"If no one would come to me, then I would go to them."

It was difficult to come down from that peak but, after about three months, I was able to resume a life within the world of time.

As it turned out, the land next door to the cabin was for sale. I was able to buy it and eventually build a home. Now I had my own expanded cabin in the forest and I spent the next few years living peacefully there. Occasionally, I ran workshops and retreats in the meditation center that I had built on the land.

I had no expectation or desire for any more awakenings. I was more than content to live a quiet and peaceful life, going for walks, sipping tea in the local cafes of Byron Bay, and sharing the teaching with those who found their way to me.

In December of 1990, I scheduled a residential retreat, once again at the Jasmine Retreat Center.

I was about to enter into my third awakening.

THE THIRD AWAKENING

It was a seven-day retreat and, on about the sixth day, once again, I began to open up into the eternal dimension of existence. If I reflect upon the earlier experiences, I would say that the first awakening was a massive opening of the heart. The second was an opening into Christ consciousness. The third was an awakening into God consciousness.

I was taken on a journey through the mystery of existence. I became the rocks and the trees and the birds and the sky. I journeyed through time from the beginning to the end and from the end to the beginning. I experienced God in everything. I felt the Presence of Buddha and Jesus and Mohammed. I was in the company of saints and sages. It was profoundly mysterious.

After several weeks, the awakening gradually subsided and it took many months of integration before I could resume a normal life.

THREE MORE AWAKENINGS

There have been three more awakenings. The fourth occurred at my home in Byron Bay in 1992 and lasted only a week. It involved revelations about the nature of love and what it means to live lovingly in the world.

The following year, I was invited to run some workshops in New York and Boston. The response to my teaching was so positive that I decided to move to America. I spent the next five years traveling from place to place. I would simply go wherever I was invited. All my possessions fit into the trunk of my car.

The fifth awakening occurred in New York City during the summer of 1994. It was an integration of all the other awakenings. As I wandered the streets of Manhattan, in a completely altered state of consciousness, everything seemed to fall into place. All the insights and revelations of my earlier awakenings collapsed into a single point. Sacred geometry arose within my mind, somehow revealing the origins of existence.

Once again, I experienced Oneness with everything I encountered. But this time it was with cars and buses and lamp posts, rather than trees and flowers and the river. Everyone looked enlightened to me. I could see that we are all brilliant actors playing out roles upon some cosmic stage.

After the fifth awakening, I was sure that it was over and that my journey was complete. I did not expect anything more and then, without warning, the sixth awakening occurred in May of 1997.

I had just finished running a residential retreat in Northern Michigan and was staying with a friend in Chelsea, which is a thirty-minute drive from Ann Arbor.

During this sixth awakening, which lasted for about fourteen days, I felt like an Immortal. I was very connected to the stars and to space. I was connected to the world of ascended Masters and to the angelic realm. I was in a continual state of rapture.

One of the features of this awakening was a profound love for animals. There was a farm nearby, and each morning, I would walk there and spend time with the geese and peacocks wandering freely around. There were also goats and very large horses grazing in the greenest paddocks. I felt so much love for them that I could hardly bear it.

One day, it occurred to me that I wanted to see other animals. I wanted to see lions and tigers and gorillas. I wanted to see zebras and giraffes, and so my friend drove me to the nearest zoo, which was about two hours away. We arrived before the gates opened and waited for almost an hour.

When at last we entered, the first exhibit we saw was that of the gorillas. They were in a large grassy enclosure. In the distance, I could see a large male gorilla standing next to a smaller female. There were also two or three young gorillas and a baby.

I walked over to the viewing area. A large glass panel provided a clear view of the gorillas, gathered together in the far corner of the enclosure. I was in a deep state of loving Presence as I stood behind that glass wall.

Slowly, the female gorilla began to walk towards me. With each step she took, I became more present. She gazed directly into my eyes as she approached and, to my surprise, she sat down right in front of me and placed her hand on the glass, as if to greet me.

I was filled with love for her in that moment. She truly was a magnificent and present Being. I placed my hand on the glass opposite hers and we entered into the deepest level of communion.

Gazing into her eyes was like gazing into eternity.

We remained in a state of silent communion for at least ten minutes. I found myself speaking to her.

"I love you," I repeated over and over again.

And then the deepest level of sorrow arose within me.

"I am so sorry," I told her. "I am so sorry for what we have done to you."

It felt like I was speaking to all gorillas through her. How could we be so cruel and destructive in our unconsciousness?

In that moment of Presence with the gorilla, I had no doubt that they are far more conscious and noble than any human living upon this earth.

The deep remorse that was arising within me was not enough to overwhelm the love I felt for her. I just sat with her, telling her over and over again that I loved her, and that I was sorry.

Our communion continued for another five minutes and then, to my amazement, the baby gorilla slowly approached, sat down next to his mother, looked right into my eyes, and raised his hand to meet mine.

I spent the next fifteen minutes, hand to hand, with mother and child. The only thing between our hands was a thin layer of glass.

Gazing into the baby's eyes was like gazing into an ocean of innocence.

After a while, other humans began to gather around to watch what was happening. They were talking and laughing and it was clearly time to disengage. I said good-bye to the gorillas and decided to leave the zoo. I returned to my friend's home and remained in an awakened state for several more days.

I have since been to Africa to witness the animals in their natural setting. I saw lions, hippos, zebras, water buffalos, giraffes, monkeys, baboons, and elephants all living harmoniously on the plains of Kenya. It was beautiful beyond imagining, but I will never forget that time I spent in Holy Communion with the gorillas at the Toledo zoo.

A FINAL WORD ABOUT AWAKENINGS

The awakenings that I have described are peak experiences and, like all experiences, they come and go. They arise through grace and they leave of their own accord. You cannot hold onto them, nor can you desire them.

Peak experiences are not necessary in the process of awakening.

For most people, awakening will be gradual. It will involve embracing true responsibility. It will involve right relationship with the ego. It will require courage and honesty to reveal every aspect of who you have become on this long journey through time and separation. You will have to empty out those reservoirs of repressed emotions. You will have to release yourself from entanglement in others. You will have to transcend judgment. You will have to open up into the truth of life, the truth of love, and the truth of power.

But the real key to awakening is to learn the art of being present, so that the present moment becomes the very foundation of your life.

Presence is the master key. It reveals the I AM of you. It reveals Oneness. It reveals the living Presence of God in all things present. It reveals Heaven on Earth. And it transforms your life within the world of time.

ABOUT THE AUTHOR

ABOUT THE AUTHOR

Leonard Jacobson is a modern mystic and spiritual teacher who is deeply committed to guiding and supporting others in their journey towards wholeness.

He was born in Melbourne, Australia, in 1944 and was educated at the University of Melbourne, graduating with a law degree in 1969. He practiced law until 1979. He then set off on a long journey of spiritual discovery which took him all over the world, from the United States to the Middle East, India, and Japan.

In 1981, he experienced the first of a series of spontaneous mystical awakenings that profoundly altered his perception of life, truth, and reality. Each of these experiences took him to deeper and deeper levels of consciousness.

He has been running workshops and seminars for the past twenty years, offering inspiration and guidance to those on a path of awakening.

He lives in Santa Cruz, California, and offers evening teaching sessions, weekend workshops, and longer residential retreats in the United States, Europe, and Australia.

He is the founder of The Conscious Living Foundation, a registered non-profit organization. In 2005, he was awarded the Peace Prize by Religious Science International, although he is not affiliated or associated with any religion or church.

He is the author of three books, *Words from Silence, Embracing the Present,* and *Bridging Heaven & Earth.*

For more information, call 1-888-367-3315
or visit www.leonardjacobson.com